WRITING IT OUT

Self-Awareness and Self-Help

Through Journaling

by

Lisa M. Schab

ii

Published by

Wainsley Press

ISBN 0-9653988-0-3

Printed in the United States

For any information please contact
Wainsley Press
P.O. Box 546
Nevada, MO 64772

DEDICATION

This book is dedicated to my husband, Bernd Harrer, whose love and support have been unconditional and never-ending...

And, to the memory of Margaret Dahl, whose spirit, encouragement, and wisdom left a cherished mark on my life.

iv

AUTHOR'S ACKNOWLEDGMENTS

I would like to thank the family of my beginnings: my parents, Betsy and Bob Schab; my grandmother, Gertrude Netter; and my aunt, Ellen Schab; for their nurturing and support of my talents, and for their love and encouragement.

I thank my chosen family, my husband, Bernd Harrer, for his patience and support.

Thanks to all of the close friends and brief acquaintances who shared their journals with me, the quotations from which helped to create the heart of this book.

And I would especially like to thank my editor and publisher, Neil H. Swanson, Jr., without whose support this volume would not have come to be.

AUTHOR'S NOTE

Throughout this book, you may notice the use of a plural pronoun (such as "they" or "them") to refer to a person of unknown gender. These words are chosen over "he/she" or "he or she" as a means of handling the lack of a gender-inclusive pronoun in the English language.

While I hope that "Writing It Out" will be helpful to most people, I want to emphasize that it was written for use by the basically emotionally healthy individual and is not meant to be a substitute for prescribed psychological or medical treatment. The ideas put forth herein are suggestions for the person interested in self-help, and they do not guarantee change.

In the introduction to Part One, I explain that this book does not provide direct answers to your problems. I do, however, believe journal writing can be an effective and enjoyable tool for you to use in the search for your own answers. I wish you the best of luck on your journey!

FOREWORD

Writing It Out is a self-help book based on the premise that self-awareness is necessary for long-term change, and that writing in a journal is a practical and valuable approach to achieving self-awareness.

The book explains why the writing process is a useful one in becoming self-aware, gives practical information on how to journal, and provides a large number of exercises and interpretations for the reader. The exercises provide an experiential learning opportunity, immediate feedback, and an effective way to learn self-questioning skills leading to greater self-understanding.

Because, for some, writing is an easier and "safer" method to promote insight than talking, the journaling approach has great value for therapists working with individuals, couples, or families, as well as the leaders of self-help groups and twelve-step programs. If personal matters are difficult to verbalize, writing can offer a more comfortable first step in identifying memories, thoughts, and feelings. *Writing It Out* can be helpful to any student in a writing class, for it offers many suggestions for practice in the craft as well as a path toward each student's personal voice as a writer. Due to its practical, inexpensive, and easily-accessible nature, journal writing is also a viable activity for the general public. Persons who would simply like to expand their self-knowledge can easily guide themselves through this book.

The author's training includes a bachelor's degree in communications from Northwestern University and a master's degree with honors in clinical social work from Loyola University. She is currently working as a Licensed Clinical Social Worker in private practice—treating individuals, couples, and families in psychotherapy; offering support groups; and providing community education. She also has a dozen years of free-lance writing experience, including a human interest newspaper column, a year as the editor of "The Capable Kid Report" (a newsletter for professionals working with children and adolescents), and has had numerous articles published in magazines and newspapers.

This book grew out of a seminar the author developed which explores the value and versatility of the writing process as a tool for self-expression, self-exploration, and insight. She has used the journaling exercises in self-help seminars and adult writing classes. As a practicing psychotherapist, she has used the seminar material with individual clients, couples, and groups. Due to the enthusiastic response of students and clients, and their request for further materials, she was encouraged to expand the original material into book form.

The book is clearly written and well organized. One of its most valuable features is the amazing variety of practical exercises which are made available in Part Two.

After reviewing the manuscript, a retired clergyman who has had extensive training and experience in personal counseling wrote: "I wish this book had been available many years ago so that I could have shared it with those who came to me for counseling. I think it effectively achieves its purpose of providing an approach which can be used by all who are interested, whether or not they are in therapy. It is an excellent way for them to come to a better understanding of themselves, and a good technique for the solving viii

of personal problems. "

A wide spectrum of people will find *Writing It Out* to be an unusually helpful book—from teenage girls to recovering alcoholics, from senior-citizens groups to college writing-students. It will be useful as a tool for therapists, teachers, guidance counselors, parents, writing instructors, self-help programs, women's groups, writers' clubs, religious organizations, camps and retreats—not to mention: etcetera, etcetera, etcetera!

Summing it up, I am extremely pleased to have become aware of Lisa Schab's *Writing It Out*, and I am enthusiastic about having the opportunity to get it published as a book.

—The Publisher

CONTENTS

PART TWO: JOURNALING EXERCISES

INTRODUCTION

There is a very important difference between this self-help book and other self-help books that you will read. In most of these books you are asked to learn about certain principles, commit them to memory, and apply them to your life. You are told that if you read specific chapters, and follow a particular set of steps, your questions will be answered and your problems will be solved. In other words, you are given answers to your questions and solutions to the problems with which you are dealing.

You will find no answers in this book.

I do not believe that answers come from self-help books. I do not believe that answers come from other people who write self-help books. I believe that the answers to yourself come only from yourself. And, I believe that you are the only one who can find those answers for and within yourself.

What I do believe this book can do for you is to provide you with a guide — a map to use on the journey to your self. I believe that journal writing can be an effective and enjoyable tool for you to use in the search for your own answers.

Within the pages of this book, you will find a number of guidelines and suggestions for using journaling as a tool for self-awareness. The guidelines are here, but the answers are not. The answers to your individual life do not lie in this or any book.

They lie within you. Keeping a journal can help you find your way to them.

The quotations from various journals are comments or excerpts from actual persons and/or their journal entries. Names and other identifying information have been changed in order to maintain the confidentiality of the contributors.

PART ONE

Journaling Guidelines

1 JOURNALING: WHAT IT IS

I can still remember the very first diary I owned. It was a pale satiny pink in color, with the words "Every Day Diary" written in embossed gold script across the cover. Three more thin swirling lines of gold underscored those words, and flowed toward the first page with a promise of wonderful, exciting things to come. I opened up the book and the blank pages before me beckoned toward what I imagined to be a magnificent future — a future filled with friendships and parties and growing up and, maybe someday, that incredible thing called "love." (This was in the days when little girls had no other ambitions save finding Prince Charming.)

The diary was a gift from my grandfather on my 11th birthday; the filling of those blank pages marked the beginning of my career as a journalist, and the beginning of my journey into adulthood.

It is no coincidence that the words "journal" and "journey" both begin with the same four letters. Deriving from the French, the word "jour" means "day," a "journal" is a diary or "day book," and a "journee" ("journey") is a day's travel or a day's work. (In the Latin before that, "dies" is the word for "day," "diurnus" means belonging to a day, or lasting for a day, and a "diurnal" is a "journal.") You will find that any diary or journal, once begun to be filled with the words of a human soul, does become a journey: a journey to one's self.

"This book I read says to write every day — a lot — about anything — to fill a notebook a month. It sounds right and

it sounds good, but it sounds scary. To expose so much of myself. To have myself on paper means that other people can read me. As much as I claim to be myself, the thought of other people reading my insides, uncensored, makes me uncomfortable. If I talk, I can censor it. I can let them see only what I want them to see. To know only what I want them to know. But if I write it all out, what if someone finds my journal and finds me? If they read it they would know so much of the inside of me — naked, unarmed, my raw soul bared, no defenses, no make-up. Like someone seeing your soul without make-up on.

But, I do feel in my gut that it would be good — that it would help to get things out of me, to help me to get to know myself, to help me find out what is inside. I like it; it's like a cleansing. I feel that I could write for an eternity about myself." -Jenny

Diary vs. Journal

The terms "diary" and "journal" are often used interchangeably. However, there are a number of ways to define these terms, and for the purposes of this text, a distinction will be made and observed throughout the book. The identifying features in this case will have most to do with the idea of structure.

When most people hear the word "diary," they are reminded either of the diaries of youth such as described above — vivid, emotional recountings of life's treasured or tormenting experiences — or, diaries somewhat less connected to the heart, kept for the purpose of simply recording the day's activities. Preprinted calendars, schedules, and appointment books also serve as diaries.

What all of these arenas for recording have in common is a definite sense of structure and organization. Dates are printed at the top of each page; times may be prerecorded, one to a line, for easy scheduling of appointments; and, most likely, there is a limited and inflexible amount of writing space allotted for each day.

This type of imposed structure can be helpful to the writer wishing to use the book for the purpose of organization and scheduling. The writer also may enjoy the limits to the amount of recording that can be done in one day. But for the purposes of journaling, which will be explored in this book, strict structure and organization are not what we are looking for.

In contrast to the diary, two of the most valuable qualities offered by a journal are *flexibility* and *open-endedness*. Journal writing is usually done in a book without preprinted days, dates, or times. There is no predetermined amount of space into which you are forced to fit yourself. There are no printed suggestions as to what or how much should be written in each day's entry. These characteristics that physically distinguish a journal from other types of writing arenas are the very traits that lend journal writing its magic, and its unique ability to encourage individuality, creativity, and self-discovery in the writer. By leaving the decision of journal entry length and frequency of writing up to the writer, the journal becomes an instrument for fostering self-trust, self-worth, and self-awareness. The unstructured format gives control to the journaler, allowing only internal guidelines to determine when and how often and for how long the writer should write.

> *"My journals are non-dated, because then I don't feel confined to fitting what I want to say on that page. I can write 16 pages on one day, or just two lines."* -Maggie

> *"My mood dictates whether I write or not. Sometimes I just feel like I want to write something in the journal."* -Daniel

A Place to Grow

A teenager's diary is a scary place. It is a sanctuary, a home, a trusted friend. In a world of other-imposed rules and regulations, and at a time in life when independence and self-discovery are at their peak, the diary offers one place where the adolescent can take refuge — one place where they may voice their opinions without censor, speak for as long as they like about anything they like, and for once, tell, instead of being told. In a diary, fears and insecurities may be spilled, and dreams and hopes may be explored.

The diary is nonjudgmental and accepting. As it becomes filled with the thoughts and feelings of the writer, it becomes a physical representation of that person, offering one of the first views of the inner self, separate and apart from parents, siblings, and friends. Through the diary, the teenager begins to learn and recognize internal qualities, and to become acquainted with that person whom they are so excitingly and painfully struggling to become.

The adult journal can offer the same benefit of confidentiality and security. When used to its fullest measure, it should provide safety, acceptance, and opportunity for expression. The journal should be a place where you can go to be truly and fully yourself.

As adults, however, journal or diary-keeping can be taken a step further. The journal can be used with a purpose. It can be entered with a goal in mind, and worked and reworked as a tool for self-awareness and, ultimately, self-help.

> *"I. Myself. Jenny. Me.*
> *I am the only one.*
> *The only of myself.*
> *The only one in the world.*
> *I am unique.*
> *The only such combination*

of flesh, skin, hair, organs, breath, life.
I am the only one like this.
The only one of me.
All that I am
is what is contained within me.
Everything I need is inside of me.
Everything I can become is within me.
All of the potential, all of the resources
are in me.
I just have to look
and see what is there.
To let myself out." -Jenny

"Another journal. My, I wonder how many I've kept through the years. Since Tom encouraged me to keep a diary as a sophomore in high school. Now I'm 31 years old and still needing to express myself on paper. It has been wonderful therapy." -Colleen

"I always laughed at diaries because it was a 'little girl' thing. But when I started doing it, it didn't seem so funny anymore. Once I started, and knew how much better I felt afterwards, I decided that this wasn't such a bad idea."
-Rich

A Place for You

Very basically, a journal is a written record — of events, thoughts, feelings, or whatever else the writer chooses to record.

The ideas put forth in this book are designed to assist you in successfully beginning the process of journal writing, and, if you desire, to also consciously reap the benefits of that process: self-awareness and the keys to self-help.

Please be aware, however, that one of the greatest joys and benefits of journal writing is simply, and importantly, the enjoyment of the process itself and the essential freedom and lack of structure which it offers. There are therapeutic benefits to be gained from the physical act of filling in blank pages alone.

If you wish to journal for pleasure, you will find guidelines in this book. If you wish to take a step further, you will also discover the means to using the journaling process as a purposive tool to become better acquainted with yourself. You will have the chance to begin to learn and understand who you are as well as *why* you are. And, should you desire, there is also the chance to begin to make changes in your life, through your patterns of thinking and behavior.

All of this is possible through the simple process of "writing it out."

> *"What I like about journaling is that it makes me feel connected to my deepest feelings — the inner me. It's an affirming process. It seems like so much of life is lived on the surface. Having a connection to the things you're really feeling adds so much to life." -Jack*

> *"Journal-writing helps me because it releases stress. It's something to look forward to. It's a way to sleep at night. It keeps me from eating. Also, I don't need to have anybody else around. I don't have to talk to my mother or pick up the phone and call a friend. I can deal with it by myself, and maybe problem-solve by myself, too." -Claire*

> *"If a personal journal has an introduction, then this is it — the place where I say what it's all about. And, what it's all about is quite simple: to record my thoughts and feelings at particular times." -Daniel*

2   AND WHY IT WORKS FOR YOU

So, you are thinking, just what is it about writing? How can the act of running words across a blank sheet of paper ever help me to figure out what secret motivations and feelings lie inside of me and cause me to do the things I do? How can using a fine point or a medium point or a felt-tipped pen and a piece of paper ever help me to understand why I cry so easily, or why I am afraid of getting a new job, or how I can have a better relationship with my kids?

In my experience as a professional journalist-teacher-social worker-student-dreamer and unrelenting-seeker-of-answers, I have found that the act of writing, and especially personal writing such as that which fills the pages of a journal, can be invaluable in the process of searching for and finding answers to the questions of yourself and your experience in this world.

There are a number of reasons why writing is an effective technique for gaining self-awareness. Benefits are found not only by examining the content of what is written, but also in the act of the writing process itself.

> *"I started writing because I thought that it would help me to think things through. I thought it would somehow make it clearer to me if I put it into words and on paper." -Erin*

Physical Therapy

Have you ever climbed up on the seat of a child's swing, let your legs dangle, and then slowly but surely began to move back and forth, giving up control to the command of gravity and losing yourself in the steady rocking motion? Have you ever fallen asleep in the back seat of a car, listening to the steady drone of wheels on pavement and the soothing hum of the engine in the background? Have you ever become lost in thought while stirring a cake batter or soup on top of the stove, or while sanding or painting a piece of wood, the continuous physical movement acting as an elixir?

The physical experience of steady, smooth, repetitive motion can act as therapeutically for you as an adult as it did for you as a little child being rocked to sleep on your mother's knee. The rhythm and tranquility of the movement relaxes you by becoming an escape hatch for tension, burdensome thoughts, and emotions.

In the process of writing, the act of putting pen to paper and feeling the pressure of the connection between instrument and page, the smooth flow of ink releasing across the surface, and the rhythm of fingers and hand traveling from side to side can serve the same purpose. When done in a safe atmosphere and in a positive state of mind, writing in a journal performs a simple therapeutic function: it can relax you.

> "It's 5:15 a.m. and my nerves aren't allowing me to sleep. Instead I'm going to write in here, then get up and run my 4 miles. It's the only way for me to deal with my topsy emotion." -Claire

An Outlet for Emotion

Inherent in the presence of emotion is its need for expression. Over time, human beings have found many ways to release feelings. Crying, laughing, talking, smiling, yelling, running, jumping, hugging, sex and violence all are outlets used daily.

Some methods of emotional release are more appropriate than others. Some are constructive, others are harmful. Some serve to solve problems, some only to create more. In each of our lives, every day, we struggle to find suitable, satisfactory, and fulfilling ways to express feeling.

The act of writing is one practical option. Putting words onto paper is an appropriate physical outlet for feeling. It is constructive, not dangerous, and can be productive.

Anger simmering within you can quickly reach its boiling point and explode with harmful results if not recognized and let out while it is still of manageable size. Have you ever heard someone say they were so excited "they could burst?" Even holding pleasant feelings inside for too long can cause stress. Adequate management of feeling states is an important social skill as well as a health measure.

When verbal or other physical expression is not immediately possible, writing can serve as an outlet for feelings. Writing the words, "I AM SO ANGRY I COULD SCREAM!!" on paper is a much safer way to express discomfort on the job than it would be to swear at your boss. Writing the words, "I AM SO EXCITED I COULD BURST!!" can be a satisfying way to share good news when there is no one else around to tell.

The journal offers an immediate, convenient place to let out your feelings. Later examination of those same feelings can lead to increased self-awareness.

> *"Psychologically, journal-writing enabled me to get rid of a lot of hate and anger that I'd been harboring for the last 25 years. In many ways it was a catalyst to get rid of this." -Elaine*

"I started a journal because I needed a place to sound off, to write my feelings down. I needed a place to put my emotional energy." -Colleen

"I think I get through a lot of anger through journal-writing. Once I was very angry about a situation and there was no one to be angry at because I did it to myself. Journaling was a way to vent it. Also, I realized that when I wrote less I got into more trouble with my anger, because I was venting it at other people instead." -Abby

A Sense of Control

Because of their intangibility and lack of concrete bounds, feelings that are allowed to exist and "float" only in your mind can, at times, appear overwhelming and larger than life. They may cause a sense of helplessness, or a feeling of lack of control.

Those same feelings, when put into words and physically placed on a piece of paper, lose a great deal of their power. Why? Because you have taken the power for yourself. You have done something with the emotion instead of letting the emotion continue to do things to you. You have transformed the abstract (thought/feeling) into the concrete (printed word), and in doing so have let the wind out of its sails.

By putting the feeling into concrete form, you have made it visible to the eye, and thus less frightening. You have reduced it to a two-dimensional entity, a group of black letters stuck to the page in front of you. You have taken something that seemed enormous and made it much smaller than yourself. The feeling no longer "owns" you because you have manipulated it. The ownership has reverted to you.

By transforming the intangible feeling into the concrete, familiar form of the written word, it has automatically been made smaller, and thus, physically more manageable. You have regained your sense of control over your feelings.

> *"Where to put these feelings, what to do with them? They seem to get bigger inside and try to burst through my skin. Sometimes they go crazy and I get scared I can't control them. But writing forces them into the pen and they come out with the ink and are captured on paper, not able to haunt me unless I read back over it. Writing chains them to the paper. They can't get up or off. I control them."* - Jenny

> *"Journal-writing gives me peace of mind. When I'm going through a lot of turmoil it seems to clarify things better when I can put it into words on paper."* -Rich

Clearing the Mind

It is likely that most everyone has experienced the kind of sleepless night where the body is exhausted but the mind won't shut down. You lie awake for hours, worrying about some event in the future, or something you wish you had done differently in the past. Perhaps you have an important decision that has to be made. The thoughts keep swirling as you turn over and over, switching from one uncomfortable position to another.

Troublesome thoughts, when left to roam aimlessly around the mind, seem to feed upon their own anxious energy. They build momentum and frustration until they become a never-ending uncontrollable circle. Now you're not only worried about your problem, but also about how you will handle your lack of sleep.

Mental strain and confusion can occur just as easily during the day, especially in a culture which values speed and volume of output. As our society becomes more complex, so do our responsibilities. The number of decisions we must make daily, as parents, consumers, employees, students, and citizens, are monumental.

The act of writing can help you to manage your information and put a break in that vicious circle. Writing out feelings and thoughts releases them from your mind and acts as an emptying process, relieving the feeling of confusion and frustration. Thoughts written on paper are more easily manipulated. They may be read and organized, put into list form, or, put away for later perusal at a time when it is more practical for you to tackle your problem.

I remember when I was a little girl, someone gave my father a "trouble dump" as a gift. The device was simply a 4 or 5 inch high silver replica of a garbage can. It came with small slips of paper on which you were to write your troubles. After you wrote down what was bothering you, you put the paper into the little can and were supposed to be free from any more worry.

The can sat on my father's desk for some time, and later became a permanent fixture in my doll house. But as I think back on it, the idea was a good one and would have provided an effective medium for "writing it out."

> *"For me, journal-writing is closely akin to letter writing. It's a catharsis, it cleanses the system, you get things out."*
> *-Daniel*

> *"I journal because it helps me put my feelings down on paper. I guess it gets things more clear for me. It helps*

me see why I'm upset and helps me to focus on what I need to work on in my life. In my mind it all kind of jumbles together, and I'm not able to focus as well." -Abby

Tapping the Unconscious

One of the greatest benefits of the journal-writing process is its ability, when done correctly, to break through defensive barriers and to tap into the material of the unconscious mind. Relaxed and fluid writing is an excellent way to temporarily annihilate strict censors and discover parts of yourself which you may not even have been aware existed.

The "conscious" is that part of the mind which you are generally aware of and in touch with on a waking basis. It is the place from which you do your thinking and talking and decision-making. Your conscious mind is letting you understand what you are reading right now. It is also telling you whether you are in a comfortable position in your chair, what color shirt you are wearing, what you will do when you are done reading this passage, and whether or not you are really taking to this whole idea of journaling.

Your "unconscious" on the other hand, is that part of your mind with which you normally are not in touch. Your unconscious is a vast collection of thoughts, feelings, and memories which affect and motivate you without your actually thinking about it. For example, you may find yourself taking a wrong turn and ending up 15 minutes late every time you drive to the dentist. Without planning to, a fear of having dental work done has diverted you from your conscious goal of reaching the dentist's office. (Your unconscious goal may have been to avoid that dentist at all costs.)

The unconscious mind is a valuable source of information for those of you wishing to increase your self-awareness. Essentially, it is a "storeroom" which holds all of the thoughts and feelings about every situation which has occurred in your lifetime. It is this material which holds the keys to who you are and why you are.

Unconscious material may be revealed spontaneously, such as in dreams or "slips of the tongue," or, it may be sought with conscious effort. Allowing the unconscious material to escape, however, requires some work on your part to take down the barriers which normally hold it in place, or repress it, from your conscious mind.

Journal-writing can be an effective tool for tapping the unconscious. When you become both physically and emotionally comfortable with the writing process, the free expression of your innermost thoughts will begin. You will be able to stop measuring your words and searching for what to say. You will no longer think about the fact that you are writing or what you are writing. You will finally get past the constraints of your conscious mind, and allow the material to flow from your unconscious and onto the paper in one fluid motion. This is where the greatest source of material is released and where you will come in contact with your true, uncensored self.

This type of writing will come more easily for some of you than for others. It will require a conscious effort to be honest with yourself and as undefensive as possible. The more you are able to commit to this end, the greater your potential for self-understanding.

> *"I started journaling for self-discovery. It was a reflective time in my life. I had a need to get in touch with an inner current of my feelings, thoughts, and impressions." -Jack*

"Journal-writing seemed to clarify my feelings about a lot of things. Since I wrote without any forethought, I wrote as the thoughts occurred to me. I found myself writing things I'd never thought before. As I was typing everything that I felt about something, suddenly a thought would occur to me, or come to the surface." -Elaine

"When I am writing, I just sit and listen and feel. The writing comes from inside of me and the feelings come from inside of me — the real gut of me." -Jenny

Acting As a Partner

An aging, yellowed newspaper clip remains tacked to my bulletin board. It reads, "Loneliness is and always has been the central and inevitable experience of every man." (Thomas Wolfe)

In the greater portion of my life I do not experience loneliness. I am surrounded by caring, loving family and friends, and I have learned to be my own best companion as well. I do not believe that loneliness is a function of the presence of other people. Some of the loneliest times I have known were those when I was surrounded by others.

Loneliness, as Wolfe suggests, comes to us by the very nature of our existence. From the beginning, we are individual beings. We both enter and leave this world by ourselves. No one realizes this separateness more than the terminally ill patient, who may be physically surrounded by other people, yet is going through a very singular experience, blatantly disconnected from loved ones no matter how closely they are held in spirit.

Connection with others provides the opportunity for social,

emotional, spiritual, physical and sexual fulfillment. It is through relationships that these needs are met and that we experience growth. These connections need not only be with others. Perhaps the most important and satisfying relationship we can have is with ourselves. It is the ability for self-understanding and self-nurturing which allows us to understand and to give freely to others.

Journal writing acts as a source for relationship when others are not available, and also fosters our relationship with ourselves. Expression of thoughts and feelings on paper offers benefits similar to verbal expression, and at the same time allows us the chance to practice a very basic form of self-help.

In this respect, your journal becomes your partner. It is there for you, always, as an outlet for your ideas and emotions and as a mirror reflecting those components back to you. In allowing you total freedom of expression, your journal provides you with a nonjudgmental ear, and becomes an arena for growth in your relationship with yourself.

(The following example is taken from the journal of a woman who was recently widowed. She used her journal as a partner over a span of time to help her through the mourning process.)

"I don't understand my calm, my efficiency, my stability. I'm handling things well. I even sleep O.K. I don't even cry much. I just keep thinking, 'This is what I should do. This is what's expected.'

"Am I angry? Some say there is anger, but I don't think so — only this terrible hurt, this pain. A physical thing, really raw.

*"The house needs re-doing. The garden needs weeding.
I should go through the photos, maybe divide them. But
first there's the papers, the bills, canceled checks, and
insurance. How do I file them? How can I remember? I
don't understand it. I must learn about it but where to
begin. What do I want and what should I do? Where am
I heading? What shall I do? I am terrified of doing
nothing. I am terrified of doing something.*

*"Push off the covers, can't sleep, pat the pillow, turn it
over, can't sleep, too hot, too tired, count backwards, doze
off, fall asleep. Suddenly awake, hot all over, panic, what
to do, where to go, how to manage, all the problems, just
can't do it, awfully hot, tossing, turning, can't sleep, fix
the pillow, get a drink, read the paper, very tired, can't
think, fall asleep.*

*"To the bottom and back but better again. How hard it is.
I expected sadness and loneliness, even the hurt and the
pain. But this roller coaster — the ups and downs. I am
determined. I pick myself up, laugh a bit, and then down,
down. Today was better. I'm O.K. now. But what about
2 a.m.? What about 3 a.m. or 4? We'll see.*

*"There is much yet to be done, bills to pay, drawers to
clean, calls to make. But I have survived another day and
there's a certain satisfaction for having done no more than
that.*

*"Laughing, joking around the camp fire. Crackers, cheese,
and other good things. Telling scary stories to the
children. All is well — at least it seems so. Seduced into
relaxing, when the sound of something quiet sets the mind
to remembering. All the defenses drop away and the tears*

*come unexpected. Bad times, good times, gentle memories
are my blanket. Not the constant lonely sinking, but some
laughing, looking backwards. Looking forward to another
way of living." -Mae*

An Accurate Record

Most people are familiar with the old fisherman's story of "the
one that got away." Each time the story is told, the escaped catch
takes on greater and greater proportions, and the struggle between
fisherman and prey becomes more dramatic. The storyteller is
victim, as we all are, of an imperfect and somewhat biased
memory.

Because our crafty memory can play these kinds of tricks on
us, distorting facts, omitting information, and skewing the details
one way or another, we are at an advantage when we keep a
journal. When we record something the first time in black and
white, it is there in permanent record for us to look back on. It
offers us a more accurate memory than does our own mind.

Having your past behaviors, thoughts, and feelings available in
written form allows you the advantage of being able to call on
them when necessary. This gives you the chance to gain
perspective, identify patterns, and assess the progress that you have
made. Rereading your journal is one way of learning about
yourself which will be addressed more thoroughly in Chapters 8
and 9.

*"Writing helps me to organize my thoughts and I like to
reread things. I'll go back and see what I was thinking at
a particular time. It helps me to understand things in the
present by reading things from the past." -Mike*

"Journal-writing gets out my thoughts, it makes me understand them more, and makes me look at them from another point of view." -Lynne

"I started a journal because I know that I can't recall things easily from memory and I wanted to keep track of events, feelings, and things going on in my life. I wanted to make a permanent record of it." -Daniel

A Change Agent

Through the process of writing in your journal, and through examination of the content of your entries, you will be able to experience an increase in self-awareness. This is a valuable accomplishment in and of itself. (The importance and benefits of self-awareness will be discussed more extensively in the next chapter.)

Some of you will want to take your journaling experience even further and use it as a tool for self-help and change. This may be done by altering your behavior patterns based on your new self-awareness, gleaned either through free form writing, with the aid of suggested exercises, or from the use of a "behavior log."

A behavior log is a structured form of journaling which will be explained in detail in Chapter 13. Its unique ability to effect change comes from the manner in which the recording is done. In a behavior log, you must keep a structured record of certain behaviors that you wish to monitor or change. One of the guidelines for logging is that you record the desire to perform a behavior before you carry it out. This forces you to stop what you are doing to write in your journal and, therefore, actually alters your behavior by interrupting it. In this manner, the act of writing serves as an immediate agent of change.

> *"Here I sit in my big couch in my red long johns, listening to music and writing. I love this time; it amazes me that these same kind of times used to make me feel so alone and miserable."* -Abby

> *"I'm becoming my own person! I didn't adapt. I cause others to respond to my initiatives."* -Mike

> *"I want to write about stifling, how I do it to myself. Never really letting go all the way. I've got to trust myself, let myself go, dare to be who I am. If nobody else likes it, too bad."* -Jenny

Putting your thoughts and feelings onto paper holds many benefits that attending to them mentally does not afford. Try using your journal as a catchment for the contents of your mind, and let it help you to increase your understanding and regain control of your behaviors and your life.

3   SELF-AWARENESS: NOT JUST WHO YOU ARE, BUT WHY YOU ARE

Self-awareness is a term which has already been used and will continue to be used over and over again in this book. It is the main goal for your journaling activity. It is the key to self-understanding, and the first step toward long-lasting self-help.

Self-awareness is, simply, the possession of knowledge about yourself. It is a conscious, informed state of being with regard to what makes you "you," and what differentiates you from your brother or your neighbor or anyone else in the world. Self-awareness is a comprehension of who you are.

> *"The journal is a place to vent things and be aware of what you're doing. It may not solve everything, but it forces you to think about who you are and how you act. It helps you to know yourself better." -Abby*

> *"So, who am I without anything else? Who am I alone, by myself? Who am I without labels, boundaries, restrictions, or outer constraints to flow in and help define me? Without them I am — a woman, female, human, frail and strong, sensitive; like film, I react easily to things that touch me." -Jenny*

Two Types of Awareness

The ability to know who you are and the ability to know why

you are, are examples of two different types of self-awareness. Knowledge of who you are involves the ability to hold truthful, descriptive information about yourself. Knowledge of why you are demands at least a basic understanding of how you came to be the person whom you describe. There are many different levels of both of these types of awareness.

For example, most people can recite certain information about themselves. We know our name, age, birthdate, address, phone number, hair color, eye color, height, weight, marital status, religion, etc. These are basic facts about ourselves which describe who we are. These facts can usually be determined by simple observation.

More careful observation allows us to describe ourselves on a deeper level. We can talk about our skills, talents, and idiosyncrasies. We may describe ourselves as, "an avid reader," "a good artist," or a "terrible procrastinator." We may say that we are musically inclined, enjoy nature, or have a fear of flying.

There is also information which is less easily observable. This includes things such as our favorite color, favorite food, dreams for the future, and how we best like to spend our leisure time. These facts involve an even deeper personal knowledge. They illustrate another level of the "who" type of self-awareness.

Most of the information given above holds answers to the question, "what?" *What* is your name? *What* is your marital status? *What* skills do you have? *What* do you like to eat? (Also, what kind of car do you drive? What type of music do you prefer? What is your occupation? What do you do when you feel angry?)

The second type of self-awareness involves more in-depth examination than even the deepest level of descriptive information.

This type of awareness allows you to understand why you are who you are — why your favorite color is red, why you chose the occupation you did, or why you are afraid of heights.

There are successive levels of this type of self-awareness also. Some people know that they went into the entertainment business because they enjoy being in front of an audience and being the center of attention. Others know that they drive a two-door sports car because, for them, the pleasure of driving outweighs the safety factor which would come with a four-door sedan.

On another level, some people are in touch with the reasons behind even these facts. The entertainer understands that he likes attention because he didn't get much growing up in a family of twelve. The sports car driver is aware that he values risk over security because his father made a lot of money in the stock market and taught him the benefits of a wise gamble.

Many people begin the journaling process with questions about their behaviors. They seek the answers to why they have such short tempers, why they can't stop smoking, or why they continue to become involved in unhealthy relationships. Finding the answers to these questions requires a commitment to self-awareness on the deepest level. This is the level which will be of the greatest benefit in helping you to make changes in your life and solve the problems with which you are struggling.

"In the morning, the sun comes in the window and looks around the room and tells me who I am: I am a soft pink sweatshirt; I am a cluttered desk. I am books upon books, and I am worn out Reeboks. I am shoulder-padded shirts and a denim coat thrown over a chair. I am an exercise bike and a Sunday crossword, and stacks and stacks of paper. In the morning I am crumpled nylons and uncashed

checks and letters needing to be mailed." -Jenny

"Listening to Marty today in her 'down' mood made me think about how I handle being down. (I don't handle it too well, do I?) When things trouble me I get quiet. If something is bothering me and I have a choice between verbalizing and being quiet or keeping it inside, I'll usually choose the latter. Being quiet also means I don't participate in arguments ('fights') very well. I usually hold my feelings inside." -Daniel

"I'm depressed today. I've not even been at my new job for two months yet and I'm already hoping for a way out. What is wrong with me? Why do I hate every job I ever had? It makes me crazy." -Maggie

"What am I going to do if the mail doesn't come? Chances are I'll cry or at least pout for awhile. My problem is that I really need feedback — almost immediate — that's why I don't want to write, because I'm afraid, and because there's no one there to tell me whether they approve or not. I've always needed that approval." -Erin

First Aid for Problems

Each day of our lives we must make problem-solving decisions. Some of the problems we face are relatively easy to solve, others are more complex. The decisions we make about how to solve them have a great effect upon our success and happiness in life. Do you know any people who seem to repeat the same mistake over and over again? They spin their wheels, never learning from or overcoming their initial problem. These people, for some reason or another, aren't choosing the best approach for solving that problem.

If we think of our problems in a medical framework, they may be seen as "wounds." Each of us has many wounds from which we suffer. In general, there are two approaches that we can use to try and alleviate our suffering: the *band-aid* approach or the actual *healing* of the wound.

The band-aid approach involves treating a wound by covering it up. Healing the wound requires mending it from the inside out. Both of these approaches will relieve our suffering to a certain extent, the first producing short-term effects, the second providing more long-term answers.

Let's look at a simple example of the band-aid approach. Suppose you have a very large grape juice stain right in the center of your white living room couch. Every time you entertain, you eliminate the spot by covering it up with an afghan. The problem is solved for the time being and nobody knows the difference. However, as soon as you remove the afghan, your problem is back. You haven't really eliminated it, you have only covered it up. This is an example of treating the *symptom* of a problem — the part that shows. This solution is effective as long as you have the energy to keep covering up the problem. However, it will never make the problem really go away.

A second example deals with human behavior. This time, let's suppose you have kleptomania — a persistent, uncontrollable urge to steal. Every time you go into K-Mart, you come out of the store with your pockets full. You aren't proud of this behavior, and remind yourself time and time again that this is not proper, much less legal. Yet, you just can't seem to stop.

Finally you decide to solve your problem by using the band-aid approach. You never again let yourself get within ten feet of a K-Mart. You treat the symptom of your problem (the behavior, stealing), by avoidance — a variation of covering up. As I said, the band-aid approach to problem-solving has a temporary effectiveness. And, as long as you can keep on with your covering up activity, you will not have to deal with the symptom of your problem.

However, the act of covering up the symptom requires a great deal of energy. It means a repeated confrontation with the problem each time it arises. I have found that in most cases, the symptom is only a side-effect of the real problem. If you treat only the symptom, the problem will keep recurring. Treating the symptom does not really heal the wound, it only covers it with a band-aid.

A second method of problem-solving involves the actual healing of the underlying wound. This method requires a greater amount of time and energy in the beginning of the problem-solving process, but it also serves to eliminate the problem on a long-term basis. It allows you to heal the wound more completely, therefore doing a more effective job of problem-solving.

Let's look at how the healing approach differs from the band-aid approach. Remember the grape juice stain? Throwing an afghan over the stain was easy and required little initial effort. However, it had to be repeated over and over again. On the other hand, had you decided to use the healing approach, you would have had to purchase a stain remover and spend some time and physical effort cleaning off the stain. This second method of working at the problem from the inside out would require more effort initially, but would also solve the problem for good.

In the case of your kleptomania, the band-aid approach of

avoiding the store worked to alleviate the symptom. As long as you didn't enter the store, you didn't steal. This didn't require too much effort, except that each day you had to struggle with yourself to stay away from that store. You had treated the symptom, but had not dealt with the underlying problem. Using the healing approach, perhaps you would have decided to get some professional help for your problem. This would have required an initial outlay of money, plus some commitment of time and effort. However, eventually you would have solved the problem and not just covered up the symptom. You would not have to deal with your kleptomania again.

Both approaches to problem solving can work. There may be times when the band-aid approach is clearly the preferred option. For someone battling gray hair, the band-aid approach of coloring the gray every couple of weeks would probably be preferable to having a hair transplant. For the person who was going to buy a new couch in a few weeks, covering up the grape juice stain would be a smarter decision than spending the effort to clean it up.

You alone must make the decision as to what problem-solving approach is the best for your situation. The more *self-aware* you are, the more insight you will have as to what it is that really needs to be changed and the better decision you will be able to make. Writing in your journal can directly aid you in increasing your self-awareness.

"Let's take a look at the main reasons why I'm depressed, shall we? 1. I hate my job. 2. I hate staying home. 3. We have no money. 4. I need something meaningful in my life, a reason to get up every morning. I know that should be my children, but I need more. I've got to get another job so I feel like I'm contributing something to this world. Well, I think I'm one step ahead because at least I know

what I'm depressed about. It would be hopeless if I hadn't the slightest idea. " -Maggie

Observation

The main method for acquiring self-awareness is through observation. Looking at statistics, facts, and watching behaviors can give you the information which you need to answer the questions of who and why you are.

Most people find the task of observation much simpler to perform on people other than themselves. From where we stand, we have a relatively clear view of everything and everyone around us and a somewhat more distorted view of ourselves. It is easier to watch other people simply because they are more naturally put into our line of physical as well as psychic vision.

Watching the behaviors of others is also less threatening than watching our own behavior. We can handle seeing things we don't like in others more easily than seeing things we don't like in ourselves. Self-observation does not always leave us with a positive feeling.

Finally, effective self-watching requires the greatest amount of objectivity possible. It demands a great deal of neutrality when making observations, and neutrality can be difficult to accomplish when looking at ourselves. Often, we are harder on ourselves than need be. (You've heard the expression, "your own worst critic.") And then there are those who find it just as difficult to admit to any of their own negative characteristics. You will find that self-observation can be facilitated by writing in a journal.

"As I survey my apartment I see clothes, dishes, piles and

piles of paper and books. My bills are sitting, my car needs work, three feet of snow is running into the basement, my bathroom sink is leaking, the oven leaks gas, half of my lights are burned out, I haven't eaten a normal diet or slept through the night in weeks, my cat won't eat, I haven't seen a lot of my friends in ages, and yet I feel pretty good. I'm not sure why I feel so good. Maybe just being in the middle of this does something to you, or you keep thinking things could be worse." -Abby

"It's amazing what the mind will do to avoid facing unpleasant emotions. As I was cataloging cassette tapes today I thought about how I have avoided playing some of them since Eve and I broke up. So many of the songs were 'our' songs. But there is no our anymore. It's odd too, the way the mind organizes good and bad feelings. The relationship's end was the only bad part. The beginning and the middle were quite good. Most of my memories of the times spent with Eve are pleasant ones. Remembering the good times doesn't fill the empty feelings I get whenever I think of her, however." -Daniel

"I'm feeling a little sick, and as I've not done anything for the last three days, it can only be nerves and pent-up emotions trying to get out. I think I've displaced all my depression of Christmas on Mark, but if he'd write a little more often I'd probably not be so depressed. I've lain here trying to write a letter for two days now and just can't. We seem so far apart and I'm really afraid to go home. I'm beginning to wonder if it just isn't Christmas and birthdays and New Year's Eve — all of which I've tried to play down in importance. I've tried to make it seem like I don't care that I'm alone. But I really do I guess." -Erin

Journal-Writing and Self-Awareness

Objectivity is most easily accomplished when we are able to get a good perspective of what we are looking at. Usually the further back we can stand from a scene, the better view we will get of the whole picture. Taking a step back from what we are watching affords us more clarity and perspective.

Because you are in the very center of yourself and your life, it is harder for you to get this perspective when observing yourself. It is possible, however, to learn to take a step "outside" of yourself. Putting descriptions of behaviors, thoughts, and feelings into your journal helps to accomplish this. The written information is evidence of who you are. Journal writing allows you to put this evidence outside of you, affording you a more objective view.

Writing in your journal also allows you the advantage of going back and re-examining facts and observations according to your needs. The written record in your journal acts as a more accurate record of your self than does your own memory. Your journal will not forget, and will not distort facts and stories over time as the human memory has been known to do.

Getting this perspective on your self-observations will increase your ability to find answers to the question "why." These are the answers which will let you understand the reasons behind who you are and the choices that you make in your life. It is this type of knowledge which is the most beneficial for self-help.

> *"I started writing in a journal to try and understand my feelings. So when I write down what I'm feeling at the moment, and then I go back and read it over, I understand how I was overreacting."* -Lynne

"Keeping a journal seems, so far at least, like a good way to sort out thoughts and put them in perspective. Or, if not in perspective, at least to state them clearly and, in so doing, organize them in some meaningful way." -Mike

"As I read back through my journal, I could see the exact time when my discontent began. I could understand it better then, and what it was all about." -Jenny

The Intrinsic Value of Self-Awareness

This chapter has dealt with self-awareness, its benefits, and the role it plays in self-help. It is important that you also understand the benefits of self-awareness not just as the means to an end, but as an end in itself. If you are relatively content with your life and don't have any major problems to solve, you needn't feel that you are wasting your time by reading this book, or by learning how to become more self-aware. There is a great deal to be gained from increasing your self-awareness no matter what your final goal.

Increased self-awareness can enrich your life in a number of ways. It can enable you to feel more sure of yourself just because you know who you are and why you are. It can boost your confidence in decision-making, and strengthen your convictions about your choices and behaviors. It can give you confidence in the path you have chosen and therefore make you more effective in your work as a musician, hair dresser, doctor, sales manager, parent, courier, or poet.

A healthy level of self-awareness can help you to conserve your emotional energy. Because you are in touch with who and why you are, you are better able to correctly assess your needs and thus, better able to fulfill them. You waste less energy making the same mistake over and over and over again. You waste less time in frustration and spend more time in constructive problem-solving. You, therefore, become more productive and happier in general.

When you are in fine tune with who you are and why you function the way you do, you are in a better position to hear messages that you send yourself. You are more sensitive to your feelings, and so are able to recognize signs of distress and need at their very first stirring. Because of this you are able to alleviate problems before they arise — a kind of preventative self-help.

The guidelines and exercises in this book are designed to help you increase your self-awareness, no matter what your goal. Just because you don't have a bad habit that you want to overcome, or an emotional problem that you need to solve, doesn't mean that you can't benefit from self-awareness in its own right. The benefits are great, and journal-writing can lead you to them.

> *"I am intense. I am fire. I am the sunlight on the walls. I am all things real and all things good. I am a part of everything around me. I am aware, I am alive. I am senses, touch and sight. I am soft and hard, wet and dry. I am light and energy. I am everything that I can open my mind to being. I am. This is who I am."* -Claire

4   JOURNALING AND THE SEXES

Sex roles — the behavioral expectations for men and women — comprise an integral part of any social structure. Traditional roles played out by parents and other adults teach young children "rules" about how they are to act throughout the course of their life according to their gender. Usually, if a role is narrowly defined it is easier to learn and understand, but it is also more limiting. A more broadly defined role offers greater choice for individual expression, but may take longer to establish because of its lack of firm boundaries.

Sex roles in American society are undergoing a great deal of change. Traditionally rigid and narrowly defined expectations for behavior by the two sexes is loosening up. Women and men are beginning to share more common ground as females take their place in the work force and men discover the more sensitive side of their personalities. This is a change that can benefit both genders, as we remove limits and allow both men and women the chance to realize a greater percentage of their individual potential.

Major restructuring of roles like this, however, can upset both social and individual equilibrium. While we are in transition, there is confusion as we explore, test out, and sometimes become overwhelmed by the new choices. With such loosely defined roles and broadening of expectations, we can become lost in the possibilities and uncertain of who we are "supposed" to be, for ourselves, as well as for the opposite sex and society. Many men these days are not sure if they will appear chauvinistic by opening a door for a woman, or rude for not opening it, while women struggle to find a realistic ground between motherhood and career.

Your journal is a wonderful place to explore and practice some of these new opportunities for expression. It is private and safe, and in it new ground may be explored and mistakes made without great consequence. In addition, the act of journaling itself can increase your ability to take on new roles as it provides an act of self-nourishment, focuses on feelings, takes the focus off of body and product, and places emphasis instead on inner self and process.

This chapter is written with both men and women in mind. It addresses issues relevant to both, and should be read completely whatever your gender, because (happily) we are finally realizing that many men's issues are also women's issues and many women's issues are also men's issues. And, the more we understand and hold compassion for each other, the better off we will all be.

"Journaling opens your eyes to the whole emotional and spiritual side of life. You really can't understand other people unless you understand yourself." -Jack

The Role of Nurturer

Traditionally in our culture, women have been assigned the role of nurturer. We were not only raised to physically give birth to and nurse our children, but also to be responsible for their emotional feeding. While the man's role has been to provide goods (money, food, shelter, clothing), the woman's role has been to provide services (teaching, nursing, sensitive caretaking.) Although these expectations are changing, many of the women reading this book were raised — from the first doll, to the home-ec class, to the job about "MRS" degrees — with the idea that their main purpose in life was to care for other people. Theconsequence of this upbringing is a society of adult females who are wonderful mothers, wives, grandmothers, social workers, etc., but who have very little capacity for self-nurturing.

You've all met the woman who cares for her children, husband, pets, the PTA, Brownies, and (finally), also holds down a job outside of the home. Her life runs without a hitch until she encounters a situation where she needs to care for herself. That's when she falls apart.

Women have always been trained to come running when a baby or a husband or a friend or co-worker cries out for someone. But what about themselves? Many women do not even recognize when they are in need of emotional nurturing. Or, if they do realize their need, they are quick to brush it under the rug — whether that means ignoring it by throwing themselves back into their work, turning the music up a little louder, or having another cigarette. Women ignore their own emotional needs because they have never learned that they have a right to them, much less learned how to fill them. Women highly capable of soothing the crying baby, husband, friend, or boss, wouldn't know where to begin to soothe themselves in an appropriate and healthy manner. Instead, they either learn to ignore their own needs, or to use inappropriate, often self-destructive, ways to fill them — (smoking, drinking, eating, spending, etc.)

If you are one of these women, your journal is a perfect place for you to begin to both recognize and accept your own needs and to learn how to take care of them. As you become comfortable with expressing your feelings, you will eventually come across feelings of need. In your journal, you do not have to ignore these feelings or be afraid of them. They are your birthright, just as all of the other feelings that you will discover and explore. And, once you learn to identify and accept them, you can also learn to fill them for yourself.

Use your journal to explore your needs. Think about them, write about them, see what they feel like. Write them out and look at them, accept them, and start to seek ways to fill them all by yourself. Being able to nurture yourself does not mean that you will never again seek solace in other people, for this is one of the greatest joys that we can give and receive from each other as human beings. But the ability to do some of that solacing for yourself is strengthening, practical, and healthy. It feeds your soul, your ego, and your self-respect — those things which are crucial to our being able to ever have anything to give anyone else.

So use your journal to learn to nurture yourself. When you are in need, write about how you would help another person if they were in your shoes. Would you help them by listening, babysitting, cooking a meal, giving them a couple of hours off, or by putting an arm around their shoulder and saying, "It's O.K."? If you would do even one of these things for someone else, then you are surely capable of, and more importantly, worthy of, taking the time to do these things for yourself. The act of writing in your journal is in itself an act of self-nurturing. Allow yourself that; give yourself that. And as you begin to recognize your needs (self-awareness), you will also begin, through a process of trial and error, to learn just how to fill those needs in the best way for you (self-help).

> *"By keeping a journal I've learned that I can get through the tough times, somehow, some way. I also learned that I wasn't such a failure. Sometimes when I wrote things down I was able to understand why and what was going on; I could deal with things myself. I didn't need other people to help me do that all the time." -Colleen*

"Do not see him. Do not see him. When you see him, he cons his way back into your life. You need a chance to breathe and explore your independence without him. You have been basing your life on him and now he's gone. You will survive this blow. You will survive being alone and without him. You said yourself that you would be fine and would find someone new. That you wouldn't sit around and wait for him or anyone else to control or rule your life. You have so much to give to someone and if you let him rule you with his inability to love and care for someone, then you deserve to be beaten. Strength, Claire. Be tough and protect yourself." -Claire

The Role of Rock

If women were traditionally responsible for the feelings and emotional sensitivity in our society, for some reason it became necessary for men to take the opposite profile. The traditional male role historically has emphasized task achievement and not only downplayed, but almost frowned upon, emotional and relationship functions. Just as women are branded "nurturer" from an early age, the little boy in our society is taught to be a builder, maker, explorer, and do-er rather than a feeler. Feelings have been women's territory, and, in more ignorant times, a man who expressed sensitive feelings was thought to be a sissy, a wimp, and certainly not fit enough to call himself a true man.

Most men in American society were raised to be "tough," to "take it like a man," and learned that "big boys don't cry." A John Wayne-type protector/provider image was presented to each little boy by his parents, the cinema, and society at large. He was taught early on that he was not allowed to play with dolls, play dress-up, or run home to mommy. A man was expected to grow up to be stalwart, and more like a statue than a real person. Men were to fight in the business world, the battle field, and on the street, and still come home each night with provisions. Flinching was not acceptable.

People raised in this type of social climate do learn to perform, produce, and provide. They also learn to ignore half of their personality and their potential as caring, feeling human beings. Emotion is what motivates us, fulfills us, and binds us together. People denied emotional expression are only half alive, and suffer the consequences through physical and mental illness.

Until recent times, it was considered unmasculine for a man to coo at a baby, express his fears, or become tearful in front of another person. Luckily for both sexes, this horrendous misjudgment is beginning to change. Emotion is now a human possession rather than a female one, and men are slowly being recognized as not only owning their own feelings but also having a right to express them without having their self-dignity threatened.

The results of this new freedom are of benefit to both sexes and society in general. More fully-expressive men are now able to show their capabilities as caring, loving fathers; to become more openly and fully involved in their interpersonal relationships; and are no longer being cheated of their emotional identities. This new attitude will enable men to develop themselves more completely as individuals; to explore and understand themselves more fully, which can only lead to greater personal success; and to recognize greater and greater potential in their lives.

Stepping into the world of emotion can be intimidating at first when you are not familiar with its many colors, characteristics, and capabilities. Emotion can seem an uncertain, uncontrollable entity until you begin to get to know and trust your own feelings. Again, your journal is a safe, convenient place to begin to explore this unfamiliar part of yourself. If you are a man who is just beginning to consider making your feelings a more valid part of your life, your journal can help you in that task.

Use your journal to practice letting out what you feel inside. Practice emotional expression on paper to help acquaint yourself with the process. Let yourself explore the sensitive part of yourself. Let it out, look at it, and become friends with it. Explore this part of you that is so important to your ability to grow into the complete person that you were meant to, and have a right to, be.

Don't worry if you feel uncomfortable at first. Don't become frustrated if you don't understand everything right away. You are discovering a new part of yourself, a very vital part of yourself. Take things at your own pace, don't push, and your emotional growth will come naturally. Use some of the exercises in this book to get you started if necessary. Your journal can facilitate your journey to your emotional self.

> *"As a boy, I was told by society that boys don't cry, don't express their feelings. My father, for example, wasn't one to express feeling. So I learned by example. Journaling has made me feel more completely alive. To take the time to open your eyes to your feelings makes your life that much fuller. -Jack*

> *"Men are raised in ways which prevent them from being emotional. We're supposed to be the strong silent type; we're not supposed to cry. We're supposed to be the one that the weaker sex can lean on. I got these messages indirectly through my environment when I was growing up — with all the guns, cowboys and Indians, and military*

games. I learned that I was supposed to be like John Wayne, strong and fearless, while my heroine would have to be rescued." -Daniel

<u>Focus Off Of The Body</u>

It only takes a glance at a couple of television commercials or magazine ads to recognize our society's emphasis on physical beauty and sexual appeal. The slogan, "Sex sells," isn't a new concept. Today the long-legged woman lying atop the car, or next to the oversized liquor bottle or behind the can of thirst-quenching soda pop is practically a part of the product. The trend is turning to include men also.

What the advertising world is telling us is that physical attractiveness is appealing. So appealing that it may be the deciding factor when choosing the products that we purchase for ourselves and our families. Because advertisers continue to use this method to sell products, it means that the concept is working. It means that for everything from two dollar tubes of toothpaste to two hundred thousand dollar cars, we, the buying public, will often enough put aside our own intelligence to purchase the product with the attractive man or pretty woman in the ad. Why? Because we want to be like them.

The emphasis in our society is on physical appearance, the body, the outer person, and although it now includes both sexes, the greatest pressure to achieve physical beauty is still on women. Since the time of Cleopatra, women have learned that they had to wear make-up to attract a man. They had to appear sexier, more sultry, and more appealing than their sister. For all practical purposes, this is still true. Our stores are filled with face creams, body creams, emollients, wrinkle erasers, anti-aging facials, eye shadows, liners, highlighters, mascaras, blushers, lipsticks, glosses, gels, hair lighteners, darkeners, streakers, removers, replacers, detanglers, perms, and conditioners. These are just a few of the products that are available for women to use — above the neck alone! — to make themselves more appealing. In America women curl straight hair, straighten curly hair, lose weight to shed curves, gain weight to add curves, wear flats to reduce height and wear heels to gain height. We wear sheers to add sensuality and wear suits to add respect.

The campaign doesn't stop at our skin and scalps, but increases in proportion when our bodies come into the picture. The emphasis — even when disguised as health — is on our weight. Thin is in, and fat is out, and fad diet markets are rolling in profits. Every year clothes models get thinner and thinner and more and more women try to shed 3, 4, 5, 25, and 40 more pounds to look just like them. These are women who are intelligent, successful, and a pleasure to spend time with. But, they don't feel enough value in their inner qualities. They believe that to be attractive in general they have to be more attractive physically.

Whether or not the current trend is on thin or fat, blonde or brunette, long hair or short, the point still remains that our society places a high value on physical looks. Although cleanliness and a pleasant appearance are definitely healthy, the overemphasis on our outer selves has been taken to extremes. We are constantly being told that unless we are thinner, prettier, have better breath, smoother legs, whiter teeth, less gray hair, and tanner skin, we are failures.

What ever happened to our personalities? What about the parts of a woman that you don't see? Her sense of humor, her intelligence, her warmth, her sensitivity, her education, her interests? The result of this physical emphasis is that as a woman learns that society values her outer self more than her inner self, she begins to do the same thing. She forgets that she has marvelous, priceless inner qualities and places her self-worth solely in her appearance. The woman believes that she is her body. This attitude perpetuates low self-esteem and self-concept, lack of self-worth, eating disorders and depression, and the idea that a woman's main value lies in her looks, which groups her more with possessions than with human beings.

Your journal is a place to begin to change this idea. By emphasizing your mental skills and emotional content, your journal will introduce you to the qualities and characteristics of your inner self. The more time you spend working with your thoughts and feelings, the more you will realize that you possess valuable components that cannot be seen by standing in front of a mirror. You will begin to know, value, and celebrate your true self, which is much, much more than a body.

If you are a woman, take a minute to think about how much time you spend each day on your looks — on make-up, hair, clothes, etc. Add it all up and come up with a round figure. Now, think about how much time you spend each day on your inner self. How much attention do you give to your inner qualities? Try opening up your journal before you put your make-up on one day. Find out who you are in the places that can't be smoothed or colored or erased. Learn to make as much time for your thoughts and feelings as you do for your body. Get to know and respect who you are on the inside, for that is where your real beauty lies.

> *"I remember the first diet that I went on was in 8th grade. I weighed 100 pounds but I thought I had to be thinner, like the models in 'Seventeen' magazine. I still stand*

sideways in front of the mirror and pick up my shirt to see how big my stomach is. I'm trying not to worry as much about my body, and say it doesn't matter if I'm thin or fat, I am attractive by qualities other than my weight." -Claire

"I have these journals. These are me." -Jenny

Focus Off Of The Product

With its fast pace and emphasis on success, our society places greater value on the ends rather than the means. Quality is often forsaken for quantity, reaching the top is more important than the experience of the trip up, and production rather than process is the overriding goal in any business venture or work task.

As Americans, our form of government offers us a priceless gift of freedom and the opportunity to become what we wish. Our society is prized for its "American Dream," and rags-to-riches stories. These are wonderful characteristics of our nation and government. But there are also side effects, felt by both men and women.

The opportunity for success carries with it the pressure to perform and progress, often pushing us into a pattern of continuous dissatisfaction. We may lose the ability to take pride in our accomplishments and instead only see the next step in front of us. We purchase a first house, then a bigger house, then another house. Then we need a boat and a third car and our own pool. All the while we continue to be dissatisfied, never stopping to consider what we have accomplished, but only to see what more we need that we have not yet achieved.

While ambition is usually a virtue, and goals for improvement are what encourage us to succeed, when we become too caught up in the future we have nothing left to gain from the present. We accept our awards with pride, put them on a shelf, and quickly begin work for the next contest, often completely ignorant of the time spent along the way — the valuable time and activity of which our lives are actually comprised. It is a great feeling to finally complete the ship in the bottle, to set it up on a mantelpiece, and bask in the achievement. But what about the hours spent at work? What about the bittersweet pleasure and struggle to fit every minute piece into place just so? What about the loving care and patience and skill which was exercised and allowed expression during the process of construction? This is what makes up the greater portion of our lives. And this is what is lost when we place all of our value on the product.

If you are a parent, or have a child in your life, you have likely been on the receiving end of a piece of primitive artwork at some time or another. There have probably been pieces brought home to you that looked like something quite identifiable — things like, "A Bird" with wings, a face, and a beak. And, there have probably been other pieces which looked like "A Mess" with no identifiable form at all.

As an adult, you probably cooed over both pieces, but picked the bird to display on the refrigerator. You chose the piece by the quality of the product. But what do you know about the quality of the process? Did you know that the bird was made with pieces that were pre-cut by the teacher the night before? Did you know that each bird that walked out of that classroom looked just the same as the others? Did you know that this was an exercise in following instructions?

On the other hand, did you know that the making of the "mess" was the one thing that made your child feel good about himself that day? Did you know that to make the "mess" he had to put his fingers into wet, cold paint and feel how soothing it was to smear it across smooth, shiny paper? Did you know that he started with both blue paint and yellow paint, but that when it smeared together it magically became green? Did you know how it felt for your child to see that huge expanse of white paper take on color and texture and meaning just by the touch of his own hands? Did you know that the "mess" picture was actually also a picture of a bird, but that in this picture, the bird was an eagle and it was flying, flying and swooping all over the paper as the child produced it? Did you know that the bird swooped down into a lake to dive for a fish, but when it got under the water it decided to stay there because it was so nice, and so the final picture is that of a bird-fish swimming happily under water?

Young children have the gift of enjoying the processes of life. The making of the picture instead of only its completion, the pouring and stirring of ingredients as well as the finished cookie, the feel of their bodies gliding through the water and not just the idea that they have swum two laps. Children have not yet learned to value product over process, and therefore they enjoy the things that make up the biggest portions of their life.

Your journal can help you to regain some of this appreciation of process over product. By making your own personal daily processes the focus of your journal writings, and by the very act of journaling itself, you will increase your awareness of the processes in your life. Use your journal to bring into focus the many steps that you take before reaching your goals. Value and appreciate those steps and the methods that you use as a representation of who you are. Use the awareness of your processes to gain understanding of your behaviors and motivations and appreciation of all the time and energy that is spent on the means to your ends.

Writing in your journal without concern for grammar or punctuation or organization of content will give you an exercise in emphasizing process over product, as will using the act of journaling itself to try and focus away from product. Don't think, "I must complete ten pages in my journal this week." Think instead, "I will write in my journal to meet my needs this week. I will write toward my goals and I will write what I need to work toward those goals." Don't think, "I must meet my journaling goals in three months." Think instead, "I will make a continued effort to work toward my goals."

As a man or a woman, be aware of the time that you spend writing in your journal — the time that you spend on your personal growth. Be aware of how it feels to express yourself and to give outlet to your emotions. Be aware of the cathartic and soothing effects of writing. Or, notice the anxiety some subjects stir within you. Take time to let yourself feel those emotions, accept them, and consider what they are telling you and what to do with them. Use your journaling time to explore the value of the process of your activity.

> *"I'm in life right now. Not watching from the sidelines, not waiting for, not dreaming of the day 'when' — I'm in it now.   Feeling, trying, struggling, hurting, loving, deserving, enjoying, pushing through, arms outstretched in front of me for protection. Making it. Going through it. Being it. Risking it. Surviving it."* -Jenny

> *"There's this new reassuring, welcoming, peaceful thing that grabs at me at certain times these days — usually upon awakening first thing in the morning, and sometimes when looking ahead to a new day. It's a pressure that's been lifted — a pressure to perform, or to live up to something. There's a comfortable, secure freedom that*

comes with the feeling that I am only responsible for myself. I don't have to live up to anyone's standards but my own." -Claire

Permission for A Personal Voice

Women who are raised to be caretakers learn to place the focus of their lives on other people. When talking with them, it is not uncommon to find that they automatically place the needs of others before their own. For most of these women, this isn't even a conscious choice. It is just a given way of functioning.

My grandmother, who is 89 years old this year, is one of the most interested and interesting people I know. She has a fabulous sense of humor, finds pleasure in every day and every situation of her life, and can hold a conversation on any current event. She is often the life of our parties and reunions.

I am always struck by my grandmother's story of her marriage to my grandfather, part of which included a change in her personality. Until her marriage, she was a great joke teller. But after she married, she stopped telling stories. "Your grandfather liked to be the life of the party," she said. "He liked to tell the jokes, and so I stopped. I was his wife, and it was my place to let him tell the jokes."

My grandmother did what she did out of love. And a great sense of obligation. In her day, women were taught to move aside and let their husbands lead. She was simply following the rules. But when my grandfather passed away, she began telling jokes again. She also painted the living room, got a new couch, and took a trip to Europe.

Today, women have been recognized as having a right to their own personalities. If my grandmother had been born a couple of generations later, she may never have felt the need to give up her joke telling. And yet, a great majority of women today are still affected by the patriarchal beginnings of our society — which is why the issues that psychotherapists so often find prevalent in their female clients are low self-esteem, and a lack of a strong sense of self. Persons who have been raised to cater to the needs of others come to value others over themselves. Other people's needs are more important than their own, their ideas are given more value, and their selves are simply granted greater importance.

These women often have trouble separating themselves from other people, and realizing that there is a place where they leave off and others begin. They do not see themselves as whole people, separate from every other person. They are so busy listening to the voices of others that they have never recognized, and certainly never celebrated, their own personal voice. Just like my grandmother. Women have even had trouble labeling themselves without using a word which implies a connection to another person, such as "wife" or "mother." (Women have traditionally been known as "Mrs. Smith" rather than "Betty Smith.")

Yes, these things are changing, but change takes time. In the meantime, it will help you as a woman to help yourself along. Don't wait for your husband to pass away before you find and celebrate your own personal voice. Don't wait for society to give you permission to have needs of your own. Start recognizing and owning those special parts of yourself now, while you've still got time to appreciate and enjoy them. Find yourself while you still have time to celebrate yourself.

Your journal is a place to discover these parts of you, to find out who you are all by yourself, without any connection to other people. Writing in your journal will help you begin to recognize yourself as a complete and valid individual with feelings, needs, and desires all your own. In keeping a journal, you begin to express the inner parts of your self on paper, capturing your thoughts and emotions in a physical form, in a central and specific place. This place, the journal, then actually becomes a physical representation of your self — something which you can see and touch — and which communicates your own reality back to you. In your journal, where you are free to express yourself honestly and deeply, you can begin to recognize yourself as a unique individual, to set yourself apart from others, and to identify the existence of your boundaries — the place where others leave off and you begin. Your journal identifies and becomes a validation of your personal voice. And, because the process of journal writing is done alone, it is a correspondence with, and acts to develop a relationship between you and yourself. You can begin to recognize yourself as a person in your own right, just like those for whom you have been caring all of your life.

> *"It's as if I've spent my whole life looking for something to fill me in. But each filling is only temporary. Friends take up some space, keeping busy, career, entertainment. But in the end, the emptiness is still there. Maybe you don't find meaning from life, maybe you have to create your own. Maybe I have to fill myself with myself." -Jenny*

> *This journal has become a validation of myself. It affirms me, that I've alive. Maybe it is a first step to validating myself." -Claire*

Don't be surprised if you find yourself identifying with problems of the opposite sex in this chapter. In healthy human beings, there are no rigid boundaries between male and female characteristics. If you are discovering and expressing your self to the fullest extent possible, you will find that you, luckily, possess characteristics which have been traditionally labeled as belonging to men, as well as those which have traditionally been assigned to women. Use your journal to increase your awareness of your own traits, whatever they may be, and to expand your ability to use and benefit from them.

5   JOURNALING MECHANICS: MAKING IT EASY, MAKING IT YOU

Up to this point, I have mainly discussed the abstract components of journal-keeping — those things which go on in your head and your heart that are relevant to the process of writing in a journal. These components are the life force of your journal. They are the parts from which and through which you will work.

In order to benefit from these abstract components, however, you must also pay attention to the concrete parts of your writing. You will never write in your journal at all if you are not comfortable with the mechanical aspects of the process. Dismissing these aspects as unimportant can prevent you from ever getting to the even more important, inner material.

You are probably aware that some physical tools are necessary for journal writing, yet you may not realize how significant the choice of those tools can be. You may think that all you need to write is a pen and paper — which is correct — but then you wonder why you never actually take that pen and paper in hand and begin the writing process.

It is true that a writing utensil and paper are the only essential materials for journal-writing. In fact, this is one of its benefits. But, the choice of that writing utensil and the paper on which you express yourself does play a part in the eventual success of your writing project.

Timing and location are also to be considered when thinking

about the mechanics of journaling. How often should you write in your journal? Where should you write? At what time of day should you write? The answers to these questions will affect the success of your journal-writing. It is important not to dismiss these considerations without a thought. They will directly affect your relationship with your journal.

Journal-writing is a very personal activity. When approached with a positive attitude, it can be tremendously energizing and fulfilling. It can soothe, befriend, and teach you. But, if you are at all apprehensive about the process, it can appear burdensome or difficult.

The point of view which you embrace will have a lot to do with your comfort level. If you are comfortable with journaling, you will look forward to it and reap its positive benefits quickly. Your journal will have a high chance of survival. If you are uncomfortable with the process, it's likely that you won't keep at it very long.

Think about the way that you handle tasks in your daily life. Which do you complete first? Which do you put off until last? Which do you never finish? Which do you never even begin?

In most cases, if you don't *like* or are uncomfortable doing something, and you don't *have* to do it, you are very good at putting it off or even forgetting about it altogether. This is why you never get around to cleaning the hall closet, going for a checkup, or visiting Aunt Grace in the nursing home. Unpleasant, optional tasks almost always fall by the wayside.

If writing in your journal falls into the unpleasant task category, you will probably treat it in the same way. But, by paying some attention to the *mechanics* of the process, you can make it as enjoyable and as comfortable for yourself as possible.

> *"I write in my room, because I'm alone there. I sit at my desk and it's dark and I put on one light. Or I'll lie down on my bed."* -Lynne

> *"I usually write in my bed or on my couch in the living room because I can relax and be comfortable and think."* -Maggie

Materials

As a writer and writing teacher, I have received numerous writing-related materials as gifts over the years. Beautiful cloth-bound journals, matched sets of silver pens and pencils, and pretty, portable "lap pads" so that I may write anywhere and at any time.

I have cherished these gifts because of the thoughtfulness that inspired them. And yet, I have used very few of them for the purpose for which they were intended.

For me to do my best writing, I must use materials which make it easy and comfortable for me to get my thoughts onto paper. My personal journal is a tattered spiral notebook with a cardboard cover. It has lines (wide, not college-ruled), it is a color which inspires me (this year's is purple), and because of the way it is constructed, it lies open flat on a table, on the floor, on the grass outdoors, or on the lumpy covers of my bed.

Depending on my mood, I write with a fine-point Paper Mate Flexgrip pen, or with a medium point Paper Mate Write Brothers pen (always in blue ink, never in black). I use ink rather than a pencil because I like the way it flows across the paper, and because ink provides me with a feeling of permanence.

The beautiful blank cloth-bound books which I receive as gifts will never be used for journal-keeping. They are every writer's romantic fantasy, and yet they are impossible for me to use. The handsome covers do not stay open for me when I try to write in them. They want to eat up my hand and pen, and I end up spending more effort trying to find a position in which I can keep the book open and write at the same time than I do in actually putting words to paper.

The blank white pages look pure and inspiring, but I like lines. I like the secure resting place they provide for my words. I like the structure and stability that they give to my shifting, unpredictable feelings.

My cloth-bound journals have not been wasted. I keep my original poetry in one, quotations in another, and particular memories in another. The writing in these books is done in short spans of time and the entries are brief. The books are kept on my bookshelf, looking very lovely and preserving valuable information.

My comfortably-worn journal, on the other hand, sits in a convenient place on the floor next to my bed. It is ready to be opened, flipped through, or written in on a moment's notice. It is easy for me to get to and easy for me to use. This makes my writing experience enjoyable; this keeps me writing.

When you begin your journal, please pay attention to yourself. Choose the materials that are right for you. I have known journalers who wrote on loose leaf paper, in 2 x 4 inch spiral notebooks, on the backs of envelopes, and in expensive, cloth-bound volumes. They have chosen #2 pencils, colored pencils, fine point pens, and felt-tipped pens.

The important thing to remember is that it doesn't matter what you use, as long as you enjoy it. Pick the materials that are your favorite, those that are the most comfortable for you. If you love the feel of your pen sliding across that giant sheet of blank paper, or if you love the sound of your pencil scratching across a yellow, lined legal pad, or, if you're most comfortable tapping away at the keys of a typewriter or a word processor, then those are the materials that will keep you journaling, and those are the ones that are best for you to use.

> *"I write with a real nice ball point pen. I always have one pen that I keep in my journal with me. It has to be smooth writing, with a nice feel to it. I'm very particular about my pen." -Claire*

> *"I like lines. It upsets me if I'm writing on clean paper and it slants downward." -Abby*

> *"I would write on blank sheets of paper — copy paper — and then I'd perforate it and keep it in a three-ring binder. The paper without lines gave me more freedom to write in any size I wanted — small or large letters, no constraint. The loose pages made it easy for me to carry. I could put the paper into a folder and take it anywhere, then put it into the binder when I got home." -Jack*

> *"I like dark ink. I don't like pencils. I like purple or dark blue ink. Ink glides better and I can read it better." -Lynne*

> *"I keep an electronic journal. I write sitting at my*

computer because I can type faster than I can write."
Daniel

When And How Often To Write

Unlike a structured diary, with a date at the top of each page and a certain amount of allotted space per entry, an open-ended journal format leaves the decision of when and how often to write up to the discretion of the journaler. With the exception of the behavior log, the time and space allotted for writing should suit your personal goals and preferences.

I once had a student who made the decision to write at a specific time each day, and for a specific length of time. This schedule was set up to discipline both herself and her family. If she hadn't set aside a specific time for journaling, she would never have found the uninterrupted time that she needed.

I have known other journalers who do not structure their writing time for the very same reason. Their schedules are such that it would be nearly impossible for them to sit down at the same time each day to write. Instead, they keep their journaling time flexible, knowing that they will fit their writing into one of several time spaces which will crop up during the course of the day.

Some journalers write before getting out of bed each morning. Some write as the last thing they do before going to sleep each night. Some sit down at the typewriter as soon as the kids are off to school, and some take their notebook to a restaurant or park every day on their lunch hour. What is important is, whatever schedule they choose, it is the one that is best for them.

I happen to keep a "write when you need to" schedule. For

me, the journal serves the purpose of expressing feelings, sometimes confusing, sometimes overwhelming. I use it as a place to write out my thoughts, both to give them expression and also some sense of order. Since this is my goal, I write simply as the need arises. Depending on what is going on in my life at the time, that could mean writing several times in one day, or not writing anything for a period of weeks. Again, what is important is that the schedule I have chosen serves my personal needs. Because this is comfortable to me, it is enjoyable and fulfilling. Because of that, I keep writing.

"I write about twice a week, mainly dictated by my emotions. Sometimes things happen that I don't want to forget; sometimes I want to rationalize something; sometimes I just write because I have the time." -Rich

"For about a year's time I wrote in my journal several times a week. I'd just sit down and write, or type 6 - 7 pages single spaced. What determined when I wrote was how emotionally distraught I was, and the availability of undisturbed time." -Elaine

Where To Write

Since the only tools necessary for journaling are paper and a writing utensil, the possibilities of where to write are many. Your journal can accompany you almost anywhere you go. Writing can be done in waiting rooms, laundromats, or hotel rooms, on beaches, trains and buses, in restaurants and in private studies. Your journal can be slipped into a purse, a brief case, a diaper bag, a gym bag, a suitcase, or a book bag.

Because of its convenience and flexibility, you are free to listen to your own needs and fit journal-writing into your personal lifestyle. Remember to think about your comfort level. Choosing a place to write which gives you a positive feeling will increase your chances of keeping up with your writing. Writing in a place which is uncomfortable or difficult to reach will decrease the amount of time you spend in the writing process.

Try to pick a place that will make journaling easy for you. You may have to compromise. If your favorite place to write is at the beach, but the beach is a half an hour away, you're not going to get much writing done — especially in bad weather. If your thoughts flow most freely when you are curled up on your living room couch at night, but your spouse always watches the 10 o'clock news, try to get your writing done before or after that time.

I find that I most often write in my bedroom, on the bed. This feels like a safe place to me. It is a place that is all my own, and a place where I can be alone. It is physically as well as psychologically a comforting place for me. This makes the writing process comfortable as well.

Choose the place that you write with as much care as you choose your writing materials. Make it easy; make it you. This will increase your chances of successful journal-writing.

> *"I usually write in bed at night before I go to sleep. Unless I'm really emotionally distraught. Then I'll go to a restaurant and have coffee and write."* -Colleen

> *"I can write almost anywhere, but I find that I tend to do it more when I have free time, like vacations, on a plane, traveling, or camping. When I'm out of the usual routine I'm a little more stimulated."* -Mike

"I write sitting at the coffee table with music in the background. It is the most comfortable place for me, and the music is soothing." -Rich

It's O.K. To Change Your Mind

The healthy human personality is not stagnant, but ever-changing and growing. Your ideas about life today and those from yesterday or several years ago may be very different. That is good. Change implies growth, and growth is healthy.

Because your ideas and values continue to change throughout your life, your behaviors will also change in reflection of this. When you first begin your journal, you may find that you enjoy writing early in the morning, and you get the best feeling using a red ballpoint pen on white typing paper. Several weeks or months later, the red pen my repulse you, and the thought of doing anything before ten a.m. may give you a headache.

That's O.K. In fact, you may find that the best writing circumstances for you change several times on a regular basis, or haphazardly. Don't worry about sticking to your initial plan! With each passing day, and with each day of writing, you are growing. Your change in preference is a reflection of your growth. Go with it.

You may need to try a number of different materials before you find those that work best for you. If you find that the pen you like to use when balancing your checkbook just doesn't make it for journal-writing, then change your utensil. If you feel like the waiter is peering over your shoulder when you write in the corner donut shop, then find a different location.

You can even turn your changing needs into an exercise in self-awareness. Ask yourself, "Why is it that I'm changing in this way at this time? What is going on in my life that might be related to this? How am I changing? What is this a reaction to?"

You can apply these questions to fluctuations in the time and frequency of your journaling entries, also. Use every behavior change to learn something about yourself. If you're unsure where to start thinking about that, write it out. The insight will come if you make a genuine effort to honestly answer your own question.

"I used to write on paper, but now that I have a word processor I tend to use that primarily." -Mike

"I like to use my computer, but sometimes what works best for me is to go in a restaurant and have coffee and write my heart out. I feel comfortable in a restaurant. The rest of the world just seems to disappear and my cup is always filled up. I never have to worry about anyone bothering me." -Elaine

It's O.K. To Make Yourself A Priority

I haven't met a (sane) person who would give up feeding their body for a week. Yet I have met hundreds of people who would exist for a week, month, a year, or a lifetime without giving any thought to the feeding of their soul. We say that we don't have time, we have obligations, or that other people must come first.

But how do you think you are going to meet those obligations and care for those other people if you don't first take care of yourself?

Just as physical energy comes from proper care for the body, so emotional and spiritual energy is derived from proper care for the soul. If you think you'll be a better parent by depriving yourself of personal time and spending every waking minute with your children, or never taking a vacation or leaving them with a baby-sitter, you're sorely mistaken. If you think you'll make a good impression by working 60 hours a week instead of the expected 40, how do you think your boss will react when your work becomes more and more inaccurate as a result of the extra stress you are placing yourself under?

The longer you deprive yourself of personal soul-feeding, the more you drain your supply of patience, understanding, sympathy, and love. The longer you go without proper attention to yourself, the more you will diminish your ability to pay attention to detail, accuracy, and quality. In short, the less time you spend caring for yourself, the less you will have to give to others.

Often people find it hard to take a block of time each day, or every few days, to sit down and write in their journals. They feel guilty because there are hundreds of other more "productive" things they should be doing: paying bills, exercising, doing housework, writing reports, or spending time with their children. Granted, these are important responsibilities, and ones which should not be put aside or overlooked.

However, the ability to give yourself emotional nurturing directly affects your ability to give it to others. As a human being trying to do a good job at life — as a parent, employee, friend, or bill-payer — you must first take some time to pay attention to your own needs. You must take the responsibility to care for yourself so that you will have the necessary resources to care also for those other people, jobs, and responsibilities.

The self-nurturing and self-awareness which you can gain from journal-writing will increase the amount of energy you have to put into producing and giving to others. Don't feel guilty for taking 15 minutes a day to spend on yourself. That 15 minutes spent writing out angry feelings at your boss keeps you from displacing that anger on the first person who walks through the door — most likely someone you love.

The purpose of your journal-writing is to do something for yourself, so make it a priority. This is a present that you can give yourself. If you can't find the time, then make the time. You deserve to benefit from journal-writing, and so do those around you.

> *"I usually write in the late evening, which may begin at 6 p.m. and run until 2 or 3 a.m. I like to write then because everything is quieted down by that time. I have a chance to relax a little, and it's a time for me. By then I've closed the business doors, finished household tasks, and it's finally my time when I can be alone and it's fairly quiet."* -Daniel

> *"Through my journal I discovered more of my own value in seeing myself in relation to others. I realized that I do have a value. I think that was something that I had to learn."* -Elaine

6   WRITING GUIDELINES

One of the most valuable characteristics of a journal is its ability to be molded and used in the manner that is most beneficial to each individual writer. I stress its characteristics of flexibility and openendedness, and I encourage you to make your journal your own, to use it according to your needs and goals and not some arbitrary standards.

There are, however, a number of guidelines which can help you to gain the greatest benefit from your journaling experience. This chapter will outline those guidelines. The more closely you follow them, the more helpful the journaling process will be in moving toward your goal of self-awareness.

> *"Feel a need to write — figure out feelings — take stock, or something.   Feeling a different feeling — a little detached, removed." -Jenny*

Confidentiality

If you went to a therapist for help with a problem, you would want to feel certain that your personal thoughts and feelings were being expressed in a safe environment. If you didn't feel that the content of your conversations would be held in the strictest confidence, your self-expression would be somewhat censored. You would probably not be able to fully voice your truest self for fear of exposure, and the effectiveness of your therapy would be diminished because of this.

The same thing is true in your journal. For you to reap the greatest benefit from your writing, you must feel free to be completely honest in your writing. You must be ready to expose the contents of your mind and heart, and to commit them to paper. This can be a scary thought for a beginning journaler! Many people are afraid that if their thoughts and feelings are committed to writing, they may someday be found and read by another person. Their inner beings would be exposed in public, and they would be embarrassed, or, get into trouble for what they had written.

This fear of exposure might affect the content of your writing. You may censor, omit, or misrepresent your true feelings and thoughts, immediately diminishing the benefits and accuracy of self-awareness which you could glean from journaling. When you censor or omit, you decrease the chances of tapping your unconscious. You also alter your physical representation of yourself, so that when you go back to read over your entries, the observations which you make will be inaccurate. Your self-awareness will be skewed, and you will have sabotaged your mission before you had even begun to reap the benefits.

I once had a student who often spoke of problems between herself and her husband. In fact, whenever we were together that was all she talked about. And yet, when she shared her classroom journal with me there was not one word written about her marital situation. She wrote extensively about her job, her co-workers, her day dreams and night dreams. But there was nothing about the biggest source of concern in her life. When I asked her about this she said simply, "Oh, I could never write anything about Jack! What if he found it and read it?"

If one of the purposes of your journal is to help you work through the problems in your life, it will not do you any good to write about everything except those problems. If, as in this case, there is a fear of someone reading your journal, you must take steps to change this situation. It seems only right that each of us should have something on this earth that is private and ours alone, no matter how good our marriage or how close our friends. If you feel that there is no safe place for you to keep your journal, then you must think harder to find a place. The trunk of your car? In your purse at all times? A briefcase left locked in a drawer at work? In a locked file box?

You shouldn't have to become paranoid about someone finding your journal. However, if the fear of someone else reading it is keeping you from reaching your journaling goals, then it is necessary to change this situation. You will never work out your marital problems in your journal by writing about your occupation.

> *"I used to have this fear about keeping a journal and committing my personal innermost thoughts to paper. I was afraid of what would happen if I died and somebody would find them and read all about me and my insecurities and imperfections and laugh at me. Well, what the hell, maybe I'll keep the juicy stuff to myself. Maybe I won't."*
> -Jenny

> *"I like writing in my journal because I can put down my real thoughts about things, what I really think. Like if I'm hating my kids at the moment I can put it in there. I use it like a psychiatrist."* -Maggie

Honesty

As I have already stated, when you censor, omit, or misrepresent your feelings and thoughts in your journal, you immediately limit the amount of self-awareness that you will be able to render from your writing. Therefore, it is important that you express yourself with as much honesty as possible.

Writing honestly means letting your ideas flow on to the paper without interruption. It means resisting the urge to structure your sentences, to make corrections, or to change what you have written. It means letting your initial thoughts about something remain as they first flowed from you, and not erasing words or replacing phrases with others that sound "better." Writing honestly means writing what you really feel and think, and not what you "should" feel and think.

The ability to be honest with yourself requires some inner strength and a willingness to be open to the truth about who you are — from every angle. It requires that you take a look at all of the characteristics which you possess, not just those that please you. It demands that you be very thorough in examining your feelings and thoughts about people and situations, and especially about yourself.

It is not unusual for people to have some trouble discovering self-honesty. As we discussed in Chapter 3, it can be more difficult to be objective about ourselves than about situations that we can view from a distance. In addition, we have built-in defense mechanisms which often keep us from realizing anything too unpleasant or painful about ourselves.

For example, let's say that you continually find yourself having relationship problems with your next door neighbors. You have moved from a number of apartment complexes because you can't stand other people's children, loud music, or cooking smells. You are tired of having to move all the time, and complain about the quality of people in your town. You can't believe your bad luck in always getting stuck next to the "idiots".

From your point of view, there are a lot of inconsiderate people out there. And for some weird reason, you keep getting assigned the apartments right next door to them. It seems to you like an incredible run of bad luck.

From another point of view, however, things are a little different. The people who know you well see you as someone who is very particular about your home and personal space. They observe how important it is to you to have a quiet, peaceful environment in which to live. They note that this is one reason you have never lived with a roommate. You don't like interruptions or intrusions in your domain.

The ability to be honest with yourself is the only way that you will gain enough self-awareness to be able to improve your situation. In this case, realizing that you just don't like living in close proximity to other people would afford you two options. You could either seek housing in a different setting — maybe renting a house of your own further out in the country — or, see what you could do to change your expectations about living near other people. In either case, it is the *awareness* of your part in the problem which will allow you to make things better for yourself.

As you become increasingly more comfortable with journal-writing, you will find it easier to fall into a pattern of self-honesty. You will begin to think less about what you are saying, and let the writing flow from within you instead. You will censor less, edit less, and write more. You will begin to trust your journal, and yourself, and find that writing will not betray you. Its revelations will not hurt you, and you will not lose your sense of control.

The more effort you put into seeking honesty in your writing, the closer you will come to your true self. Honesty is a stepping stone to the self-awareness which is necessary for self-help.

> *"Journaling made me take a look at myself and my relationships. You can't be dishonest with a journal. If you're dishonest, it's a waste of time and paper."* -Elaine

Description and Detail

The journey to yourself is like a treasure hunt. You are uncharted territory waiting to be explored. Self-awareness is the hidden treasure that you seek. The key to success in any treasure hunt is persistence and the aid of a good treasure map.

Writing in your journal is a means of writing your own treasure map as you go along. As with any map, the more detail that you have, the easier it will be to follow the map and to find the treasure. The more information you are given about the territory, the less wrong turns you will take, and the less time you will waste trudging down wrong paths.

Therefore, writing with as much description and detail as possible will help you to best understand what your territory looks like, and what you are all about. The more facts that you provide about yourself, the more accurate your map will be, and the easier your journey. The better you can describe your thoughts and feelings, the more you will know about what is going on inside of you and what makes you tick.

Think about what it's like when someone tries to describe to you a person that you have never met. If they tell you the sex of the person, you will get a vague picture in your head, but there won't be much focus. If they tell you how tall the person is and how much they weigh, you can begin to form an outline. If they tell you the color and length of the person's hair, their eye color, and the shape of their face, you can get a clearer picture. The more detail you are given about their physical appearance, the more accurately you can imagine this person, and the greater chance you would have of recognizing them on the street.

However, you still don't know much about who this person is. What is their occupation? What are their hobbies? How many people are in their family? Where do they live? And, what are they like on the inside? What kind of a personality does this person have? Are they shy, friendly, chatty, withdrawn? Are they giving, reserved, funny, serious? To really have a full description of this person, you need even further detail.

Try to keep this in mind as you write in your journal. Try to write using as much description and detail as you can. Always see if you can take a thought one or two steps further than its initial statement. If you write, "I was upset today," don't just leave it at that. Explain that statement further. What does "upset" mean to you? How did you act? How did you feel inside? What precipitated the feeling of being upset? How long did it last? When did it end? Did it feel like anything you'd felt before? How did it cause you to act?

If you were really given a treasure map, and all it had on it was the name of the country and a red "x" somewhere in the middle of the page, you would be extremely frustrated! You would think it impossible to ever locate the treasure with such limited information. You would demand names, routes, locations, directions, and landmarks. And you would be smart in doing so.

In order to understand yourself, you need to provide just as many clues as to what is going on inside of you. Asking yourself questions, and digging deeper and deeper for information, will help you to find what you need to increase your self-awareness.

> *"I feel lost. Am I overreacting to his neglect? Is it really neglect? Or is he exerting independence, or is he just deserting me?*
>
> *"I am angry. I am hurt and want to pay him back for making me feel miserable. I will not put myself out for him anymore. I am sick to my stomach. I am so angry that I want to cry out loud. He's taken my caring and has twisted it — contorted my feelings and has left me with sad, confused thoughts.*
>
> *"How am I going to handle the way I feel? How am I going to stick to my guns this time and not let my sadness or loneliness get the best of me?" -Colleen*

Concrete Images

As we discussed in Chapter 2, the act of writing takes free-flowing feelings and mental images and places them onto paper. Intangible things are given visible form, changing the abstract into the concrete. Emotions become words, ideas become sentences. This allows you to see your inner self from another perspective and gives you a greater feeling of mastery over the things that lie within you. The better you are able to place these images from your mind onto your paper, the easier it will be to examine them and learn from them. It may initially seem difficult to describe an intangible concept in concrete terms, but the more you practice, the easier it will become.

To help you in this process, begin by thinking about your five senses. These are the means by which you are aware of tangible items. You use the sense of taste, touch, sight, smell, and hearing to give you information about your environment and its contents. Think about description in terms of these senses.

What would your feeling look like if you could see it? Touch it? Smell it? Hear it? Taste it? Would it be pretty, ugly, soft, scratchy, fragrant, putrid, loud, melodic, sweet, or sour? Most of us are familiar with the description of jealousy as the "green-eyed monster". Try to picture yourself coming face to face with your own feeling. What would it look like?

Poets and songwriters have long made use of simile and metaphor to bring the abstract into the concrete and to give their ideas substance and color. Both simile and metaphor are figures of speech which make a comparison. A simile uses the words "like" or "as"; a metaphor does not. For example, the statement, "I felt like a giant next to her," is a simile. "I am a giant next to her," is a metaphor.

Animating your feeling, or comparing it to something else in the physical world can help you to get an understanding of what meaning it holds for you. Is it more like a roaring lion or a furry bunny? Would it look like a field of daisies or a stormy sea? Would it sound like a Brahms lullaby or a jack hammer?

As you write out your feelings, you are bringing them from the abstract into the concrete, helping you to realize control over them. In your writing, try to give those feelings concrete characteristics. This will help you to understand their significance and how they are affecting you.

"There's a calmness these days. An openness inside me, ready for whatever happens, waiting to see what life brings

— waiting to absorb it and live it and go with it. I feel like a sponge, just waiting for the water to run in so I can soak it up." -Jenny

"Pain so hard and deep in my stomach I almost can't write. Like I've been kicked in the gut with something invisible. Kicked in the gut and the pain spreads through all the inside of me. It eats up everything inside until I'm hollow, except for my heart." -Claire

Process vs. Product

When you are asked to write a report, or to write a letter, or to write an article, the product of your efforts is important. You must be appropriately informative, include specific points, and present them with clarity. You must use correct punctuation and grammar, pay attention to style and organization, and remove excess wordage. Confusing or lengthy passages must be edited and reworked.

When you are writing something that someone else is going to have to read and comprehend, it is essential that you communicate your message clearly. This is why children are taught English skills in elementary school and why politicians use speech writers and why celebrities hire ghost writers to tackle their autobiographies. It is important to communicate your thoughts correctly in order to be understood by your audience.

In journal-writing, however, things are a little different. It is still important to communicate your thoughts clearly, but there is much less emphasis placed on the finished product of your writing. In your journal, grammar, punctuation, spelling, and organization are all up for grabs. Paragraphs don't need indentation and dialogue doesn't need quotation marks. As long as you yourself can read what you have written and understand the meaning of your words, it doesn't matter that your verbs don't agree or that your sentences are incomplete.

The emphasis in journal-writing is placed less on the finished product, and more on the writing process itself. The qualities mentioned in Chapter 2 — physical therapy, outlet for emotion, mind-clearing, increasing control, tapping of the unconscious, and acting as a partner — are all benefits which come from the process of writing. If you keep this thought in mind as you work in your journal, you will be applying your energy where it will help you the most.

There is one exercise that I use in my writing classes which always initially throws students for a loop. I ask them to write in their journals for a certain amount of time on any topic that they want. The only guideline is that when they write, they must begin at the very far left edge of the page — to the left of the red line which runs vertically down the paper.

Oh! Their reaction is severe. How could anyone write to the left of that special line? It's unheard of! From the way they react, you would think I had asked them to commit a mortal sin.

This exercise is intended to help the students free themselves from the usual rules and regulations of writing, and in doing so, also begin to free themselves of a greater form of prescribed behavior: socialization. This can be a hard assignment to complete.

From the minute we are born, we begin learning the rules of right and wrong, proper and improper, the things we may do and the things we may not do. How many times do you remember your father or mother warning, "We don't comb our hair at the table," "We don't eat mashed potatoes with our fingers," or "We don't wipe our noses with our sleeves?"

Thank goodness our parents taught us these things. They are social patterns that we pass on to our children from generation to generation. They are necessary in an ordered society. It is important that we learn to wear clean socks, express our emotions appropriately, and drive on the right (correct) side of the road.

However, there are times as adults when it is also beneficial for us to cast off those constrictions, disobey those rules, and eat mashed potatoes with our fingers — so to speak. Certain rules, when done in an appropriate place and at an appropriate time, can and should be broken. Your journal is the perfect place to do this.

In your journal, you are free to forget about the product of your work, and enjoy instead the process of doing it. In your journal, you are encouraged to give up the rules and constraints of adulthood and let the unsocialized, uninhibited you come forth. Your journal is a safe place to "let it all hang out". In fact, the more you let hang out, the more beneficial the process will be.

Casting off the restrictions of proper social functioning can let you regain the spontaneity and creativity which flowed so freely from you are a child. Do you remember the story about the moon being made of green cheese? Of course you don't believe that now, but allowing yourself even to entertain the thought forces open the doors of restraint and sets free the child and the dreamer within you. It is that mind set which will allow you to write from your heart, and to discover the roots of who and why you are.

When you write in your journal, forget about the product of your writing. Concentrate instead on immediate expression. Try to write from the uncensored heart and soul of you, putting on paper whatever flows from you, without constraint or regulation. Enjoy writing as one of the few places in life that you can let yourself go like that.

When you stop thinking about what you are going to say, or how it is that you should be saying it, then you will start saying the things that will be the most beneficial for you to hear. When you stop worrying about the product of what you are writing, you will begin to reap the benefits of the journaling process itself.

> *"What I like about writing in a journal is that it is uncensored. I can say and write anything I want and it's O.K. It makes me feel better too, just getting it out — my anger, my love, anything. Also, there is no judgement made on my writing, except by me, if I want to make it."*
> *-Colleen*

Trust Your Gut

Self-trust is both a guideline and a goal for the journaling process. It is one of the crucial factors in developing and maintaining your relationship with yourself. Confidence in your gut level feelings and faith in your own interpretations and answers to questions is necessary for development of a sound self-awareness and self-help program.

When you take a class, or seek advice from an expert, you must believe that your instructors have a mastery of their subject matter. You must believe that the information they are giving you is accurate and true to the best of their knowledge. If you have trouble understanding something, you want an instructor to be both available and skilled at helping you to see things more clearly.

In a self-help program, you are your own instructor. You are the one who must provide the truth, the clarifications, and the answers to your own questions. This might sound like a ridiculous or impossible task, but as I stated earlier, I don't believe that anyone but you holds the answers to who and why you are. I can give you some keys to finding those answers, but you are the only one who can provide them.

For this reason, it is important that you learn to trust the information that you find within yourself. As you write, and as you read back over your feelings and thoughts, listen to your gut. Deep inside you are simultaneously expressing and responding to yourself. What comes out of you and how it makes you react is your key to self-awareness. Become sensitive to the slightest change in your feelings, and use those observations to learn about how you live and how you act and react.

Trust your instincts, your first thoughts, and especially your feelings. Trust the material which comes from within you as the reality of who you are. Trust the answers you provide to your own questions as the truth to why you are. If you are genuinely attempting to be honest with yourself, the answers you reap will be honest also.

These are the guidelines to writing in your journal. The next two chapters will provide information on how to look back and use that writing in order to learn about yourself.

> *"Day dreamed, tasted food, looked out the window, during break and lunch instead of reading. Needed to fall back after such an active week. My emotion will 'speak to me' if I choose to listen." -Jack*

"The more I write, the more I express myself; the more I express myself, the more I learn about myself; the more I learn about myself, the more I write, etc. It's the key to my soul because it's an expression of feelings." -Claire

7 READING YOURSELF: FOCUS ON FEELINGS

Expressing your thoughts and feelings on paper provides you with a physical record of your inner self. Because this record exists separately from and outside of you, it allows you the opportunity to take a step back and view yourself from a distance. This perspective offers a greater chance for objectivity and accuracy in the task of examining who you are.

I call this method of observation "reading yourself", because that is exactly what you are doing when you read back over the contents of your journal. You are looking at your insides as they are represented by words on paper, just as you would look at your outsides represented by reflections of light in a mirror. When you look into a mirror, you can tell that your hair color is blonde, your teeth are straight except for one on the bottom, and your jeans are faded at the knees. When you read over your journal, you can tell that you always seem to write when you are scared about something, you harbor a lot of anger toward your cousin Fred, and you are the happiest on days when you do the cooking.

There are a number of different ways to observe yourself, and a number of focal points which can make the process more beneficial. This chapter and the next will introduce you to some basic concepts of human behavior and provide you with a number of guidelines to help you interpret and learn from the contents of your journal.

"I have manic and depressive phases. Some days I'm really down and some days I'm really up. When I go back to read over my journal, I can see that more apparently."
-Maggie

The Importance of Feelings

Feelings are the first concept to be discussed with regard to reading yourself, because they are by far the most important. Feelings are the motivation behind your behaviors. The choices that you make in life, from what shirt to wear to what occupation to choose and the way that you behave, are all influenced by how you feel on the inside.

Most of us are aware of the fact that we have feelings, and can cite one or two examples of times when they have made our life either comfortable or uncomfortable. Some of us can remember times when feelings have gotten us into trouble. Many of us can remember certain significant events in our lives that were permeated by deep or intense feeling—weddings, funerals, births, achievements, competitions, winnings, and losses.

In general, however, most people do not pay as much attention to their feelings as they could. They ignore them, repress them, are embarrassed by them, hassled with them, and spend a lot of energy in trying to cover them up. In our culture, we perpetuate this way of dealing with emotions by labeling them as "good" and "bad." (Happiness and love are good and just about all others are bad.) We give our children messages such as: "You have no right to be angry," "Don't feel sad," and "What do you mean you're bored?"

This labeling of our feeling states as good or bad, and right or wrong, teaches us that there are some emotions which deserve expression and others which do not. We learn to admit to our happiness and to hide our anxiety, fear, anger, confusion, guilt, sadness, and even boredom for fear of social repercussion. One important fact to remember about feelings, is that no matter howhard we work on repressing or denying them, feelings will not just disappear. Neglect does not magically eliminate feelings. They will remain with us until they find an outlet of expression in one form or another. And usually, the longer we try to hold back our feelings, the more destructive they will be when they finally do surface. The result is an adult population with rampant ulcers, migraines, high blood pressure, heart attacks, and waiting lists a mile long at mental health and counseling centers.

The alternative, of course, is not just uncensored spewing forth of raw emotion. Feelings need to be expressed, but in an appropriate and healthy manner. Feeling angry at someone is a legitimate right; physically striking that person is the wrong way to express it. Being nervous before a big event is natural; smoking a pack of cigarettes in response to that anxiety is harmful. Rather than teaching only the expression of "good" emotion and the repression of "bad," we should be teaching the appropriate expression of all emotion.

For this reason, feelings should be a focal point of your journal-writing time. *Awareness* of your feelings is the key to reading yourself and understanding your behavior. *Acceptance* of, and learning new ways to express your feelings, are the keys to changing your behavior. Labeling, acceptance, and expression are three steps in learning to deal with your emotions appropriately. Your journal is a safe place to begin doing so.

> *"Exploring the whole realm of feelings was a process of discovery and exploration for me, because it was sort of*

virgin territory to me." -Jack

"I started writing in a journal to try and have a better understanding of just what I was feeling at the time—to get my feelings out on paper and work them out." -Elaine

Labeling Your Feelings

If you were asked to name the first three emotions which came to your mind, which ones would they be? Most people respond with "angry", "happy", and "sad." Can you come up with any more?

Although you may think that you know pretty much about the feelings that you experience each day, most of us are actually limited in our ability to label our emotions precisely. We use the words "happy," "angry" and "sad" to cover the majority of our emotional states. Although these are three of the most common feelings we experience, they are far from specific enough to accurately describe what is going on inside of us most of the time.

Take a minute or two to add to your list of feelings. See how many you can come up with right off the top of your head. (This will be easier if you write your answers down on paper.) When you are done, compare your list to the one below. Do you have as many? Are they are varied?

FEELINGS: happy, angry, sad, shy, aloof, proud, fearful, content, involved, correct, depressed, compliant, mad, suspicious, introspective, superior, lonely, frustrated, friendly, confused, anxious, weak, trusting, attractive, hurt, pained, suffering, bright, curious, sexy, strong, docile, spontaneous, distant, blank, rigid, arrogant, crazy, bemused, satisfied, embarrassed, silly.

All of the above words describe something that you could feel internally at any given time. There are quite a few more feelings that were not included. Yet, despite this extensive list, most of us stick to the basic "happy", "angry", and "sad" to regularly describe our emotions.

It is important to become familiar with the definitions of as many feelings as possible, so that you can begin to recognize the difference between the emotions that you experience. If you weren't sure of the meaning of any of the feelings in the list above, get out your dictionary and look them up. Most people are surprised at the great number of feelings that they never think about, or never realize that they have experienced.

Recognizing and correctly labeling your feelings is a crucial step to becoming self-aware. The more finely-tuned your skill of labeling your own feelings, the more accurately you will be able to understand and correctly attend to your needs and your behaviors. Although "happy", "sad", and "angry" are three of the most common terms, they really aren't precise enough to help you increase your self-awareness to the degree that is possible.

Feelings come in a wide range and variety, and each broader definition can also be refined to describe its many subtle variations. For example, the Funk & Wagnalls Standard Handbook of Synonyms, Antonyms, and Prepositions lists twenty-one synonyms for the word, "happiness." They are: blessedness, bliss, cheer, comfort, contentment, delight, ecstasy, enjoyment, felicity, gaiety, gladness, glee, gratification, joy, merriment, mirth, pleasure, rapture, rejoicing, satisfaction, and triumph. Each of these terms is in some way different from the other.

It would be possible to add more details, but I think you get the point! When you say that you feel "happy," is that what you really mean? How about "sad," or "angry?" The book has similar listings for those words, as well as a plethora of others.

You may be thinking, "So what if I don't know the exact distinction between 'fretfulness' and 'worry'? What does that have to do with journaling?" As I stated earlier, feelings are the motivations for behavior. Therefore, the more accurately you are able to label your feelings, the greater your awareness will be of what exactly is going on inside you, and why you choose to act and react the way that you do.

I once knew a student who very often used the word "bored" to label her feeling state. In fact, she was bored so frequently, we began to wonder just what was really going on with her. She had an interesting, full life, good friends, a busy schedule, and yet she continually described herself as bored.

After a look at this woman's journal, we discovered that bored was the only feeling other than happy that she ever assigned to herself. Through further discussion we realized that she was using the word bored for every emotion other than happiness because she unconsciously felt that to be anything but happy was bad. She had been raised to be grateful for what she had, accept her lot, and never complain.

A positive outlook is good for us all, but not to the exclusion of other emotions. What happened when this woman was angry or anxious or uncomfortable? "Don't worry about it," "It'll go away," "You have no right to be mad," "You should be thankful for what you have," were the answers she had been given as a child. And, "What's the matter with you—you're not smiling?" was the question repeated over and over.

This woman learned not to express any other emotion than

happiness. When she felt something else, she ignored it, swept it under the rug of her subconscious. The acceptable label that she finally settled upon for all of her feelings other than happiness was "boredom."

Inaccurate labeling of feelings leads to inaccurate interpretation of problems and inadequate attempts at solutions. As long as this woman thought that boredom was her problem, she repeatedly failed at solving it. Once she began to see that she was actually feeling a number of other emotions, she was able to deal with those each individually, appropriately, and with result. Correctly labeling your feelings is the first step toward dealing with them.

> *"I have decided to try and keep a diary while I'm going through this if I have time. A few notes on what I'm feeling before starting. A lot of ambivalence, which I think has a lot to do with the changes in my personal and social life mainly because of the commitment. I'm also excited. I like the idea of entering this field, and I think I'm good at what I do. I'm scared about the hours and commitment and can only guess at what lies ahead. I am feeling a lot of stress, but I'm going through a lot of changes along with this. At this point I almost feel like this will be a stabilizing factor in my very messed up life. And, I can always quit." -Abby*

Accepting Your Feelings

The second step in dealing with feelings is acceptance. It is important to learn to accept the feelings that you find within yourself. You may not like them, and your goal may be to change them, but you will not be able to deal with them at all until you accept that they exist within you.

Because many of us have been raised without a lot of training in handling feelings, we automatically shun them. We believe that they are our enemy, something to be avoided at all costs. We know from our experiences that feelings can hurt us, they can embarrass us, they can get us into trouble, and they can get in the way.

If this is your attitude toward your own feelings, one of the first things that you will need to do is to stop seeing your feelings as your enemy. Feelings are not something to be fought, repressed, ignored, or feared. They are a very important part of you—a part that deserves respect, acceptance, and expression. Your feelings are what make your personality and your experience of life different from everyone else's. They are what make you you, and not the guy next door. Your feelings should be treasured, nurtured, and allowed expression in an appropriate manner.

In order to value your feelings in this way, you will need to stop labeling them as "good," and "bad." Of course there will always be some feelings that you like and some that you dread. But try to *accept* all of them. Try to rethink your reactions, and begin to tell yourself that your feelings are important—even those which make you uncomfortable. Realize that there is nothing wrong with anger, sadness, or other "negative" emotions. You have a *right* to feel them. You have a *right* to experience a full range of emotion in your life. This is what fills you up on the inside. This is what makes you a complete, whole human being. Tell yourself that feelings are O.K.; feelings are natural. Try to accept them no matter what they are.

If you are afraid that accepting your feelings might make them more powerful or frightening, you may discover that just the opposite is true. Very often, the acceptance of feelings tends to take a good deal of the wind right out of their sails. Trying to suppress any emotion makes it seem twice its actual size. Suppressing emotions fuels their fire; expressing them releases their energy. If you are depressed and think, "I have no right to be sad, I have my health and a loving family", you may only become more depressed. You may think there must be something wrong with you if you have all of those wonderful things and you still feel sad. Accepting your sad feelings can allow you to look at them, deal with them, and get on with your life.

I once had a friend who lost his wife to cancer. Immediately after her death, he threw himself into activity. He joined clubs, got on committees, and developed a social life which never left him a spare moment. The behavior he chose kept him from feeling his sadness and depression over his wife's death—for awhile. It also kept him from progressing through a healthy mourning period. Some six months later, this man became very ill. He developed intestinal problems, loss of appetite, and didn't leave his house for three months. The entire time that he was confined to bed he spent crying and feeling sad over the loss of his life partner and best friend of 40 years. Eventually the man returned to normal health. But he most likely could have saved himself a great deal of this agony had he only dealt with his emotional pain at its onset.

When a loved one dies, it is healthy to be sad! Something very precious has just been lost. There will be a great emptiness where that person used to be. Accepting the fact that you are hurt greatly by this loss will allow you to cry and reminisce and let out your pain. Accepting it will let you eventually recover.

Many people also have trouble accepting anger, but the same principle applies. It is not wrong to be angry when you have been cheated, abused, misrepresented, or lied to. When someone does you an injustice it is natural to be mad. Accepting the fact that you are fuming over the situation will enable you to deal with it constructively.

Remember, feelings are valid. They are yours to possess, to enjoy or to be uncomfortable with, and to call your own. By recognizing or labeling your feelings, and accepting that they exist, you will be adequately prepared to give them expression, which is the final step in healthy management of feelings.

> *"Sometimes I don't know what I want. Susan says, in an offhand manner, that this is O.K. But it sinks in. I tend to think you should know what you want, and it's a sign of immaturity if you don't." -Jack*

> *"Returning home this year brought back a flood of memories of the time spent here last year with Amy. Almost everything and every place made me think of her. Facing those feelings was tough. But it was something I had to do. I feel better for having done it." -Daniel*

Expressing Your Feelings

It is in the expression of feelings that people generally run into trouble. They either don't express them at all for fear of negative consequences, or they express them inappropriately because they lack the necessary skills to do otherwise. Either of these situations is unhealthy, but can be changed with a little thought and practice.

We have already discussed the consequences of repressing your feelings, and the fact that pretending they don't exist will not make them go away. Feelings do not simply atrophy from lack of use! Instead, they tend to grow bigger, and continue to seek an escape route. Often, if they have been repressed for too long, the escape route eventually used is inappropriate and can be destructive.

Continually suppressing your frustration at your sister may cause it to come out at an innocent bystander—your child, or a salesclerk. It might turn itself into depression or a stomach knot. The safest way to deal with feelings is at their onset.

It is in the expression of emotion that we finally need to be careful and discriminating. This is where judgment calls can be made. This is where "right" and "wrong" comes in. The mere existence of a feeling is neutral, and it is acceptable. But the manner in which you choose to express that emotion can be judged. Feeling rage at another person can be warranted; taking out that rage by being physically abusive cannot. The way in which you choose to express your emotion, rather than the emotion itself, is what can be labeled as right or wrong.

How you choose to act on your feelings is also important to your own progress and growth. If you feel depressed, allow yourself to accept it, and then decide to sit and wallow in it for weeks on end because you have a "right" to be depressed, you are being no more productive than if you tried to deny it. After labeling and accepting your feelings, you must then make a decision to deal with them constructively.

One of the best ways to keep yourself expressing emotions appropriately is to increase your repertoire of expression techniques. Most people do not realize that there are almost as many ways to express feelings as there are feelings which need to be let out. You probably use these methods every day without realizing it.

Verbal expression is one of the most commonly used outlets for emotion. Think about how much you talk each day. Every time you have a conversation with a friend, co-worker, or family member, you are letting out feeling. Even if you don't plan to discuss a specific problem, your general conversation allows you to express your opinion on a variety of subjects.

The physical act of talking is cathartic in itself. If you tried to go for one day without speaking, not even to yourself, by the end of the day you would feel the pent up emotions within you struggling for an outlet. Chances are, the first person that you bumped into the next day would really get an earful.

Talking to yourself about a specific situation is a very safe way to let out your feelings. Saying, "I'm really burning up over what so-and-so did to me—it wasn't nice, it wasn't fair, it didn't feel good", lets you express your legitimate feelings of anger and hurt without having to worry about anyone else's reaction. Just the verbalization of those feelings can release and reduce the tension within you. It can let you breathe more freely. It can take away the knot in your stomach. Talking to a neutral party can also serve this purpose. Be careful not to use your conversation as a gossip session, however, and choose your listener with discrimination.

You may decide to express your feelings by talking directly to the person who caused them. This is often the best way to change a repeatedly destructive situation, or to nurture a good one. If you are going to communicate your feelings in this way, be careful to choose a time when you are sure you will be able to express yourself calmly and clearly. Feelings let out in the midst of emotional heights can often be too highly charged to be either accurate or constructive.

Physical activity is another common and appropriate form of emotional expression. How many people do you know who clean house furiously when they have something on their minds? The exertion which is required of scrubbing, polishing, sweeping, etc. is a great outlet for builtup emotional energy.

Some people choose to jog or walk or swim, play tennis, racquetball, or other sports to release emotional energy. They may exercise regularly to allow for a continuous regulation of emotional buildup, or they may schedule their exercise time according to their daily needs. Even getting out of the house or the office to take a walk around the block is a great way to relieve emotional stress. Exercise lets you express your feelings through a constructive physical outlet. Usually by the time you have gotten around the block, or completed a match, or swum a few laps, you have cooled down enough to be able to face your situation more objectively and constructively.

Verbal and physical expression are two of the most common healthy ways to express emotion. There are also other activities that can let out feelings either consciously or unconsciously. Some of them are more harmful and some are more healthy than others.

A car is a common place for people to let out emotion. Do you know someone who always drives very fast, even if they're not in a hurry? Some people keep a running dialogue with other drivers, cursing and finding fault with them, telling them how they should be driving. Do you know someone who constantly twirls their hair around their finger while they talk? Or someone whose foot is always tapping a mile a minute? Some people cry easily. Some always seem to be moving around, not able to sit still. I have a friend who laughs a lot. Yes, he's a happy guy, but his laughter also serves to diffuse a lot of other emotions which build up inside of him.

Some people drink alcohol to let out emotion. Some smoke cigarettes or eat. Some use drugs. Some always seem to be angry or agitated, always complaining and finding fault. Some people are very "huggy". Some throw themselves into their work. Some strike out physically or verbally at others.

Unhealthy expression of feeling, or that which is harmful to self or others, is usually "displaced" emotion. Such people are not dealing with their real problem. They are not aware of what is really troubling them, and are treating their symptom rather than getting at the root of the situation. They are ignoring or repressing their real feelings, and instead the feelings are being expressed in some other, ineffective, inappropriate manner.

Recognition and labeling of your feelings is self-awareness. Finding your own healthy ways to express them is self-help. Your journal is a place to become aware of and to explore your feelings. It is a place to practice labeling them and accepting them. It is also a safe and appropriate place to express them.

As you write, try to focus on your feelings. Express not only facts and behaviors, but the feelings behind them as well. Write about the different ways that you can express your emotions without being destructive to yourself or others. Some of the exercises in Part Two of this book can help you to do this.

> *"I usually use writing as an outlet. When my life is difficult, I write in my journal daily. Lately, I hardly write in it at all. Instead I write letters to friends and get things out that way. Or I release the emotion directly at the person to whom I'm feeling it, like my mother or my husband."* -Colleen

> *"I'm more comfortable putting things on paper than verbalizing. I'm a writer more than a talker, at least with personal things. It's always been easier for me to put things on paper than to verbalize."* -Daniel

8 READING YOURSELF: BEHAVIOR

Observation of your own behavior is a second method of "reading yourself" and increasing your self-awareness. Looking back over the entries in your journal and examining your actions and reactions to daily life will help you to learn about who you are. As mentioned in Chapter 3, this is self-awareness on the first level.

Self-awareness on a deeper level comes from looking beyond the surface at those same behaviors. It means seeking the connections between your behavior and your feelings. You can do this by exploring the *reasons* why for your behavior, examining *patterns* of behavior, and searching for the *roots* of those patterns in your behavior of the past as well as the present. The most important thing that observation of behavior can do is lead us to our feelings. And, as has been stressed already, feelings are the key to self-awareness.

For some of us, the task of finding and dealing with our feelings is easier than it is for others. Some people express emotions frequently and openly. Others are less aware of their feelings and may need help even in locating them. I once had a writing student, Al, who kept a journal, but never wrote about his feelings because he declared that he "never had any." He never even thought about them at all. He wanted to know why this was so, and where he could find his feelings.

After taking a look through Al's journal, we found that sure enough, he never mentioned a feeling at all, but instead wrote about behaviors. He recorded what he had done, what he was going to do, and what he wished he could do. But, there wasn't one mention of how he felt about any of these activities, or what he felt while he was doing them, or even how he ever felt in general.

This did not mean that Al didn't have any feelings! It simply meant that he had not learned how to put his finger on them. He wrote only about surface events—direct observations of his own behavior—the first level of self-awareness. To find his feelings, Al needed to proceed to deeper levels. He needed to look beyond his behavior and find out what had motivated it, to find the feelings that were behind it.

There are a number of ways to proceed to that next level of self-awareness. This chapter will suggest several methods for discovering and exploring the feelings that lie behind and may motivate your behavior. You can apply these ideas directly to the contents of your own journal. Use them as you look back over your previously written entries, and also as guidelines to lead your thoughts as you write. They will assist you in understanding not only who you are, but also why you are.

> *"It's 8:45 a.m. and I was realizing last night that I'm not writing enough—only the things that happen, but no reactions to them. So I decided to crawl back in bed this morning and do a little reacting."* -Erin

> *"My therapist wants me to write about my feelings and what triggers them, about the way I feel when I am compulsive. God, I find that difficult. I don't want to. I'm feeling anxious, nervous, I'm afraid.* -Colleen

Asking the Question "Why"

The three letter word, "why," already mentioned in Chapter 3, will be more beneficial to you than any other word you will use in relation to your journal. This question can be applied to any behavior or situation, and can be used over and over again to dig deeper and deeper into yourself and your unconscious. It will guide you beyond the words you have recorded to the inner roots of the person who recorded them. It will help you to discover the reasons you do the things that you do.

When we examined Al's journal, we found that he wrote frequently and at great length about his hunting and fishing trips. He would describe in vivid detail the experience of tromping through the woods with his dog, or tracking a fox on a crisp winter morning. One could practically see the trees and the sunlight on the snow, and almost hear every crackling step of Al's trek through the woods.

But although he could recreate his experiences in words and evoke feelings in his readers, Al always drew a blank when asked about his own feelings. When we used the question "why?" to help locate the emotions connected to his words, we began to learn a great deal about the motivations for his actions. Al discovered that he did have feelings after all; he had just never known where to find them.

When exploring your behaviors with the question "why?," you must begin at the very beginning, and work your way from there step by step. The first question I asked Al was why he continually chose to write about hunting and fishing.

"Because I do a lot of it," he answered. "It's something that I know well."

O.K., then *why* do you spend so much time in this activity?

"Because I enjoy it tremendously; it's a great pastime."

And, *why* do you enjoy this pastime rather than stamp collecting or golf?

"Well, because I like to get out in the wilderness."   And *why* is the wilderness so appealing?

"It's a wonderful escape.   It's peaceful, relaxing, clean and fresh."

And *why* do those qualities appeal to you?

Because it's a switch from being trapped behind a desk all week.   In the wilderness I can do what I want.   I don't have to listen to my boss and I don't have to worry about obligations.   I have freedom and control."

Ah ha—bingo!

The behavior in question is hunting and fishing.   The feelings which motivate it are a feeling of being trapped and out of control. Al uses this activity as a healthy antidote to his 9 to 5 weekday job. It gives him a chance to be unrestricted and playful and to forget about his responsibilities.

We did locate some of Al's feelings.   They were there all along, just hiding behind his behavior.   He doesn't choose hunting for any arbitrary reason.   It fulfills a need in him, just as a professional athlete or a construction worker might prefer a hobby which allows them to sit quietly for awhile.

You can use the question "why?" to learn more about anything that is written in your journal or anything at all about yourself. If you are wondering about a behavior or situation in your life, open your journal, and write down what you are thinking about. Then write the question "why?" Record the first answer that comes into your head. Then ask "why?" again. Let each answer lead you to another "why?" and let each "why?" bring forth another answer. Listen to what comes from within you. Trust it and believe it. This is who you are. These are the answers waiting for you; all you need to do is ask.

> *"My emotions/anxieties have much to tell me. Why do I worry about potential failure to meet deadlines instead of celebrating how much I have finished? I find myself hoping friends won't call since it will be a burden. Everyone wants a piece of me; I retreat. It's O.K. to feel this way. Why, though? What are my needs that are not being met? Need for security? Need for stroking?" -Jack*

More Questions for Looking Beyond the Surface

There are additional questions for self-searching that can help lead you to your feelings and to the reasons behind your behavior. They will help you to look at what you have written from a new angle, and will help you to think some new thoughts about the information that you have expressed. You may use these questions after you have written a passage in your journal to give you a stepping stone for deeper exploration.

Question 1)   "Out of all this writing, which sentences or passages 'move' me the most? To which thoughts do I feel the strongest reaction? What parts do I react to from my gut?"

As you read back over your journal entries, make an effort to pay very close attention to your reactions to what you are reading. Listen with a finely-tuned ear to both your heart and your body. Be extremely sensitive to any reactions you have, either physically or emotionally. Listen for twinges, tingles, lumps in the throat, tensing of the muscles, and blinking of eyes. Be aware of uneasiness, fear, and discomfort, as well as relief, relaxation, and self-confidence which you might experience in reaction to reading your own thoughts.

You will find that there are some words and passages that you will skim quickly, not paying much heed to, and there will be others that will trigger something within you, forcing you to read them word by word, causing you to feel something physically or emotionally. As you read through your entries, listen for those reactions. Ask yourself, "What part of this passage is just words to me, and what part hits a nerve, hits home, hits the mark? What part affects me on an emotional level?"

There will always be one or two areas that affect you more than others. These are the areas to take a second look at, to concentrate on. These are the areas which have the ability to teach you something about yourself. These are the areas that are important to you, the areas that you have issues with. Knowing what is important to you tells you something about who you are.

> *"It's interesting to read back over these last seven months of entries since I met him, and to see the progression of my feeling for him. Right now I'm wondering about the ability of our relationship to work. I feel bored; and then as I read, I wonder how much I am the cause of that boredom, and not him?" -Jenny*

Question 2)   "Why is this important to me? What does this subject (or person or event) mean to me? What is the significance of this issue in my life?

You may use this question as a follow-up to the first group, or you may use it as a beginning question in itself. Think about the information that is written in your journal. Ask yourself why you have addressed this particular issue, and not another. Ask yourself what meaning this subject or person or event has to you, and why is it significant? Write down the first answer that comes to your mind. Trust it. It will tell you something about yourself. If it doesn't tell you enough, ask the question "why?" again.

Let's look at an example to illustrate this process. Let's say that Mark has read over his journal entries of the past four days, and finds himself reacting very strongly to the passages where he has written about his new girl friend, Sue. He has also recorded thoughts and feelings about his job, softball team, and best friend, but none of these elicit the knot in his stomach that the discussion of Sue does.

Mark concludes that Sue must be very important in his life right now, even though he has known her for just a short time. He asks himself, "Why is she so important to me?" and writes down the first thing that comes to mind, which is, "Because she's the prettiest girl I've ever dated."

Mark's next thought is, "Wow, I didn't realize that looks were that important to me." He writes that, and follows with, "I wonder why that is. What does it mean to me to have a pretty girl friend?" The next thoughts that come to him are, "It means that *I* must be something special to be able to attract her. That boosts my ego. It makes me feel better about myself. Especially with the guys on the softball team, who are all better athletes than me.

They may all be able to hit and run better than me, but when Sue is there watching from the sidelines, it doesn't seem to matter as much. "

It's no great revelation to learn that a man is attracted to a pretty girl. But Mark has learned something more. He has learned that he feels somewhat insecure around his softball teammates. And, that it is Sue's looks, not her moral support or friendship, which he appreciates about her presence at his games. This may alert him to taking a closer look at his real motivations for dating Sue. Does he really enjoy her company, or is he just using her looks to build his reputation with his teammates? How does that relate to the knot in his stomach when he reads back over the passages about her in his journal?

After Mark becomes aware of these feelings, he checks them out by paying closer attention to his behavior with Sue on their next few dates. He realizes that he spends more time looking at her than he does listening to her. He also chooses places to take her out by thinking of where he can best show her off, rather than where either she or he would most enjoy going.

Through additional journal writing, Mark discovers that the knots in his stomach are caused by guilt. Although Sue is a nice girl, he's not very interested in her hobbies or her line of work, and he had actually guessed all along that he was only dating her for the sake of his own ego. Once he becomes aware of his true feelings, Mark can make a choice about what actions he will take now based on his awareness. He can continue to date Sue, and continue to feel guilty, or he can begin looking for a more compatible girl friend.

By the simple process of questioning himself, Mark gained self-understanding, and was able to use that information in future decision-making. Another area that he could begin to explore from here is the insecurity that he feels with his softball teammates, and why he doesn't have this problem in the work place.   Self-questioning can take you as far as you want to go.

> *"Jeannie has quit. I'm pretty upset. She's not talking about it—she's leaving for Florida to be with her parents. It's very difficult to have to face the reality of someone actually quitting. I'm both angry and sad, and scared, since all of us think about it from time to time. It also makes me realize something about myself and all of us—the lack of intimacy. I think people are afraid. Here we spend maybe 80% of our lives around this place, and yet we're not close. This is a terrific source of loneliness." -Abby*

Question 3)   "How does this make me feel?

This is, obviously, another question designed to help you become more in touch with your feelings. It is similar to asking "why?" about your behaviors, but it is worded more directly, and can help you get to the point more efficiently.

Although you already are aware that you want to try to focus on your feelings, it doesn't follow that the awareness will automatically bring those feelings to light in your writing. It can be helpful to use the concrete act of writing the question, "How does this make me feel?" to actually trigger the answers within you and allow you to bring them to your conscious mind.

You can ask, "How does this make me feel?" about any behavior or situation that you describe in your journal. You can ask, "How does this make me feel?" about anything that someone says to you, or the way they act toward you, or about any aspect of your relationship with them. You can ask this question about your accomplishments, your failures, your daily life activities, or special events. You can ask, "How does this make me feel?" about something that has happened, something that is happening, or something that only might happen.

Ask this question about even the seemingly insignificant events or situations in your life. It isn't unusual for us to be unaware that certain things that are said or done to us affect us very strongly. We tend to hide this information from ourselves because it may be uncomfortable, or because it may mean that we must think about making a change in some aspect of our lives. Ask this question about any area of your life that you wish to know more about.

When you want to find an answer to this question, write it down in your journal. Then, without pause, continue to write, recording the first thoughts or answers which come into your mind. Try to describe your feelings using detail. The more you can write about them, the better you will be able to understand them. Asking, "How does this make me feel?" will lead you beyond the events in your life and the behaviors which you act out, to the feelings which surround those circumstances and actions.

> *"Cindy and I talk about 'racing' into a relationship, building it up too much in our minds before it has a chance to develop; as Linda says, hitting a home run before you even get up to bat. It is a relief to discuss this. Why a relief? Because it is mutual. We can acknowledge our attraction to each other, yet also give ourselves more time to grow as individuals and in our knowing each other. This eases the fear that I am going to 'blow' the relationship (and get hurt/feel inadequate). (Do I feel that I am inadequate if I don't pursue a relationship as quickly as possible?)" -Jack*

Question 4)   "When have I felt like this before?

This is a question which will help you connect your present behaviors and feelings to their roots in the past, and will also help you begin to look for patterns in your emotions and actions.

Think for a minute when you are reading over your account of a situation or feeling. Ask yourself whether or not you can remember experiencing this same feeling at any other time. Does it sound familiar? Ring any bells? Trigger any memories? Write about any answers that come into your mind.

Knowing your own history can help you to understand who you are today. Maybe you have a fear of heights, and when you ask yourself, "When have I felt like this before?" you recall an instance as a little child when you were stuck at the top of a ferris wheel. Think about this connection. Understanding the past can help you make changes in the present.

It is only natural for a small child to be frightened of being stuck at the top of a ferris wheel. But now you are an adult. You have an understanding of the rational world and how it works. You know that realistically, you will not fall out of a tenth story closed window just by standing and looking out of it. You can trust the architect and the construction workers to have made this building safe for you. You needn't be nervous about the height anymore. (Of course realization and change don't always come this simply, but they can be achieved.)

When you think about other times that you have felt a certain way, you may come up with a number of examples. At closer examination, you may begin to see a pattern emerge. Patterns of behavior or feeling also tell you a great deal about who and why you are. Ask yourself if this is a common experience for you, or is it new? The benefits of discovering patterns will be discussed further in the next section.

"Been a pretty emotional day. I've broken down twice crying because of my fear about seeing my father. I still feel like when I was a little girl wanting his approval. I wanted him to think I was wonderful, cute, and adorable. No wonder I'm nervous!" -Colleen

"The story I keep coming back to is the one about my childhood. About losing the father I never knew, to the abusive one I never liked, to a mother with many husbands, and a brother always in trouble." -Maggie

The Big Picture

Having your "insides" recorded on paper separates them from you and allows a better view of yourself. It allows you to see the big picture of your life more clearly, observe your behavior patterns, and become more sensitive to every step of your progress.

Reading back over your journal can give you a new perspective on your situation. It can show you the forest when you keep bumping into trees. It can also point out particular trees when you refuse to get close enough to look at them. Reading over journal entries can pinpoint for you the exact date that something began—a feeling or a relationship for example. It can help you to see which event or which person triggered which feeling or reaction in you. These things are easier to observe on paper than to try and recall in your own memory.

Having a running record of your behaviors enables you to look back over time to seek out patterns. Finding patterns, or consistent repetitions of behavior and feelings, is an excellent aid to self-awareness. Your journal will also allow you to see the individual components of your patterns—their triggers, duration, side-effects, and endings. Armed with this information, you have the tools that will let you make decisions about what reactions you wish to take. You may decide to change your behavior pattern, and can do so by changing one component of it. Or, you may wish to leave the pattern as it is, or increase it, or alter only one part of it. None of these steps are as effective without first, realizing that the pattern exists, and secondly, knowing what it is comprised of. Your journal holds those answers for you.

Let's say that as you read back over your journal entries, you see that you seem to get along best with your spouse after a day when you've gotten some physical exercise. This observation may help you to remember to make your exercise a priority, especially if things are tense between the two of you. If your journal reveals that you always make more mistakes at your job on mornings after you've worked overtime, you may decide to ease up on the overtime so that it doesn't defeat its own purpose. The recognition of patterns such as these is self-awareness. The action that you choose to take is self-help. The knowledge about yourself arms you with information that allows you to make educated decisions about your behavior.

Once you have started to become more self-aware or to make some desired changes, rereading your journal can also provide encouragement by increasing your awareness of the progress that you have made. It is common for discouragement to set in when we feel that we have made the same mistake for the twentieth time. We think, "I'll never be able to change." In reality, however, you probably are making changes. Quality change comes slowly, and sometimes imperceptibly at first. But when you can look back at what you wrote a year ago or six months ago and compare it to where you are now, your accumulated progress will be more clear. Your journal is proof positive that change is taking place; you can see it there in print before you.

Remember, self-awareness is valuable progress in its own right. Even if your behavioral changes come slowly, an increase in your ability for self-observation or in your sensitivity to your feelings or needs shows advancement! Don't expect miracles in your journal. But, if you are at all committed, do expect results. Compete only with yourself, and celebrate every tiny step that you take. Each one is a step closer to your goal.

> *"My therapist suggested that I keep a journal so I could be more aware of my life's progressions. I can go back and read over and see the changes in my value systems. It keeps me from making the same mistakes twice, and I like noting that I'm actually accomplishing something. It's a record of my life." -Rich*

> *"I flip back constantly, just to see where I was a week ago, a month ago, to see if I've solved any problems." -Abby*

Blueprints For Behavior

When a tiny baby is born into this world, it is pretty much a blank slate with regard to patterns of behavior. Yes, it will quickly begin to cry when hungry, wet, or in pain, but the greater portion of the behavior patterns which it will develop and integrate into a personality are not yet present. There may be a predisposition to certain tendencies, but most of its individual behavior traits are yet to be learned.

From day one, the baby begins his training in behavior. He

learns which actions serve to fill his needs and which are ineffective. Initially, he finds that if he cries, he receives care. And so, he learns to repeat that behavior. As the days and weeks go by, he learns other behaviors that elicit responses in his environment. He discovers that when he gurgles a sound similar to "mama" or "dada," those two big people upon whom he is dependent for his survival become ecstatic, showering him with hugs and kisses and googly eyes. And so, he repeats those words. (Conversely, if his mother and father went into the same state of euphoria when he gurgled, "bah, bah" or "moo, moo," it is those sounds which would be reinforced and which he would learn to repeat.)

The baby's needs eventually become more varied and complex. Soon he learns that if he finishes his vegetables he can have dessert, and that if he finishes his chores he will get an allowance. He finds that if he is nice to people they will generally be nice back to him, if he drives after drinking too much he is placing his life in danger, and if he doesn't express his difference of opinion to his boss in a rational, calm way., he will come home and yell at his dog.

These are all examples of learned behaviors. If we realize that most behaviors are learned, we see that they can also be unlearned. It is because of our ability to change this way that self-help becomes possible.

The "blueprint" for many of the behavior patterns which are a part of you as an adult had its beginnings in your early learning experiences. Chance are, if you had the time, and a perfect, photographic memory, you would be able to trace most of your behavior patterns back to their earliest beginnings. You would be able to find the roots of your personality, and the reasons for your likes and your dislikes and the major decisions that you have made in your life. Since you have neither the time nor the memory capacity to undertake such a task, you can be content instead to allow the question, "When have I felt like this before?" guide you to present self-awareness through your past.

A journaling student of mine named Mitch was working in his journal on a problem that he found repeatedly in his relationships with women. It seemed that when he was dating a woman of whom he was particularly fond, he would have a very difficult time leaving her at the end of the evening. As soon as the time neared when they would be saying goodbye, he became almost clingy, and kept finding excuses why they shouldn't end the evening just yet. Sometimes he found himself physically holding on to the woman, not wanting to let her go. In his rational mind, he knew that he would see this woman again, but in his heart, he felt like their parting was much more consequential. This pattern repeated itself whenever he was with a woman whom he felt he would like a serious relationship with.

Through the process of examining his past life, Mitch began asking himself "why?" questions, and looking for times he had felt the same way before. Had there been a time in his earlier years when an important woman had left him? Although his parents had a stormy marriage, his mother had never left her children—except to go out of town on business. Wait, he thought. And then Mitch remembered the fear which he had felt as a little boy, each time his mother left, afraid that she might not return. A little child does not know what a business trip is, only that their parent is leaving. They do not know what three days in Cleveland means, only that their mother is going away. Three days? To a toddler, three days has no meaning. The only meaning is that their mother is leaving them.

Through exploration in his journal, Mitch was able to

understand and finally change his behavior. He was able to stop reacting from the little boy within him, was able to label, accept, and understand his feelings, and then finally move on. He no longer needed to react from the child he once was, but could alter his behavior to react as the adult whom he had become.

Another student came to a similar understanding about the roots of her current occupation. As a child, Allison found that she could escape her parents fighting by sitting in her room with her headphones on, listening to music. Music became a source of comfort for her, a kind of security blanket. The music could be counted on, even when her mother and father could not. Eventually, the woman became a radio disk jockey. Her friends marveled at her courage for speaking to thousands of people over the air each day. Yet Allison felt more comfortable in her studio than anywhere else, sitting again with her headphones on, surrounded by music.

Although it isn't always necessary to do an intense exploration of your childhood in order to understand who you are in the present, being open to writing about the past can be very helpful in your quest for self-awareness. Many of the root answers to the question, "why?" lie in your early years, when patterns and personality were being formed. This is one area which can be comfortably and safely explored within the pages of your journal.

A number of the exercises in Part Two will ask you to do some thinking about your past. These are designed to help you discover the root of your behaviors, so that you may use your self-awareness to actually solve your problems, rather than to merely cover them up.

"My family 'ethic' of each person making it on his own using his/her talents is taken by me to mean not asking for

*help, putting pressure on myself, and linking self-esteem
with performance." -Jack*

The Child You Were/The Child You Are

Along with recognizing and learning from the child you were
many years ago, your journal is also a safe and appropriate place
to allow yourself to express the child that still lives within you
today. Although most of us have been successfully socialized to
control the child within us, that little person is nevertheless still
present with us at all times. Your journal is a good place to
familiarize yourself with that special, important part of you.

The child within you now is the part of you that gets scared or
mad or jealous over something that your rational adult mind
realizes may be legitimate, but shouldn't be expressed the way a
little child would express it. Most of us have learned to suppress
our child at these times. The last time your boss asked you to stay
late at work for an hour, I'm sure you didn't stamp your feet and
cry, "No! I don't want to! I want to go home!" Although, you
may very well have felt that way inside.

The last time your biological children exasperated you, drained
you of your energy, and led you to the very end of your rope, the
child within you may have been thinking, "O.K., I'm not going to
play this game anymore. I'm tired of being a parent. I'm going
home." But, you probably didn't do that. As an adult, we all
have acquired resources which allow us to keep functioning in an
appropriate and constructive manner, even when the child within
us wants to take control.

That little child, however, shouldn't be ignored completely or
repressed. He or she can be a valuable source of information for

us, for they are usually very open with their feelings, just like a real child is. They will cry, giggle, or scream as the feeling strikes them. They are also generally very in tune with their needs. If your little child inside is tired of playing the parent game, listen to it. Respect its feelings by being aware of the needs that it is expressing to you. Maybe it's time for a vacation. Maybe it's time for grandma to take the kids for a day. Maybe it's time for some "you" time—to go for a walk, sit down with a good book, see a movie, or, write in your journal.

The child within you should be accepted and respected, just like your feelings. Your journal is one place to safely let that child come out and play (or scream or cry, etc.) You can pout and have tantrums and wish to be taken care of in your journal, and there will be no repercussions—except that you will feel better for having expressed your needs.

Allowing this part of yourself to come out in your journal lets you look back at and get to know that little child in you better. This is an excellent way to get in touch with your feelings and needs, which the child expresses so easily. As you read back over your writing, look for evidence of that little child. Then, pay close attention to what he or she is telling you. What is it saying about the things that are going on inside of you? Listen to and write about the answers. They are another effective key for learning about yourself.

> *"It's frightening at times. Life. Risk. Opportunities taken. It makes me want to crawl under a blanket and cling to the familiar. It makes me wonder what I'm doing! So much new these days, I have to take special time to pause and regroup. I want to cling to childhood and chicken soup and structure. Old times I used to know so well." -Jenny*

9 DON'T GIVE UP YET! — SOME COMMON JOURNALING STUMBLING BLOCKS

I have tried thus far to stress the ease and flexibility of journal-writing. I hope you are getting the idea that journaling is an activity that just about anyone can master and enjoy, mainly because of its lack of structure and rules for play. Although I have suggested some guidelines that will help you to get the most out of your writing experience, these are meant solely for that purpose, and not to use as a measure of "correct" or "incorrect" journaling.

Please remember, *journal-writing is not an activity which can be done "right" or "wrong!"* The benefits of journaling will come only when you pay attention to your individual preferences, strengths, needs and goals. You may end up writing in a manner that is more or less beneficial to you, but in general, there is no way that you can fail at journal writing.

Among those of you who have past experience with journaling, there are some who may be doubtful of this fact. You may be saying, "Can't fail? Well, I tried keeping a journal a couple of years ago. I wrote in it for three days in a row and then never picked it up again. That's not failing?" Or, you may say, "Can't fail? Well, listen to this: I tried to write in a journal once, and I found out that I didn't have a thing to say! I couldn't write a word! Now don't tell me that's not failing!"

Yes, I am going to tell you that neither of those examples constitute failure in my book. My first suggestion would be that you may have hit a stumbling block and that you should give it another try, perhaps at another time, or in another manner. If consistent, repeated attempts at journaling continue to bring about the same results, then I may think that journal-writing just isn't your thing. But, I wouldn't categorize either of those situations as failures.

The fact is, that although journal writing may be without many restrictions or regulations, it is a human activity like any other. Just as there are times when the greatest chef will burn a roast, when an Olympic diver will belly flop, or when a respected actor will forget a line, so, too, there are times when the most prolific writer will have nothing to say. There will also be times when that chef wants to be taken out to dinner, when the diver goes on vacation to the desert, and when the actor refuses to watch television, movies, or go to the theater. We all get bored with even our favorite activities once in a while. Journaling is no exception. What is important to remember is to see those little breaks in progress simply as bumps in the road, not as reasons to end the journey.

In this chapter, I have outlined some of the most common stumbling blocks to journal-writing. These are situations which have perplexed many writers at one time or another, and which, with a little patience and effort, can be overcome. If you have ever felt that you have "failed" at journaling, or feel that you are unable to get started now, I encourage you not to give up yet. Instead, read through the following suggestions, and see if you can't get back on the track by practicing a few simple exercises designed to break through those stumbling blocks.

"I always seemed to have to write in a new notebook. Because I always started writing journals when I was going to change my life, so the new notebooks signified the new

leaf I was going to turn over.   I never kept up with it at all." -Erin

"A long time has passed since I last wrote.   I've thought about doing it many a time, but just passed it off." -Colleen

Common Block 1: "I don't know where to start."

Often, one of the hardest stumbling blocks that you will encounter—and once it is overcome, you may find that it's the only one you'll ever meet—is the block of wondering where to begin. Have you ever noticed that some people enter a swimming pool by walking into the room, heading over to the side, and just jumping in?   And then there are others who need to appraise the area thoroughly, find a place to lay their towel, survey the ladders, steps, deep and shallow ends, test the temperature with their toe, and ponder the benefits of diving versus wading before they ever get into the water?

People begin journaling the same way.   Either way is fine, as long as you eventually start.   Just as you will never get any exercise or fun from swimming if you never get into the pool, you will never reap any benefits from journaling if you never begin to write.   If you want to take your time and think about the writing process for a while, that's O.K., but make sure it's only for a while.   Don't let wondering how to start keep you from actually starting.   If you find that you have had your new journaling pen and notebook for two weeks and are still spending time thinking about the great journaling you are going to do and the great insights you are going to reap, but you haven't yet actually taken off the pen cap or put any ink to paper, it's time to give yourself a kick.

It is common for prospective journalers to worry about finding the "perfect" place to begin their journals. They ponder the benefits of starting with their earliest memories, or recording the events of their day, or writing only about the most important things in their lives. This kind of thinking may seem to serve the purpose of organization or goal-setting or outlining for a better finished product. But, when you find yourself spending all of your time planning and none of your time writing, then the only purpose it is serving is procrastination.

If this is your situation, you need to change it now. The best way to do that is to pick up your pen and just begin to write. There are no rules to journaling, remember? You can't do it "right" or "wrong." And so it follows that there is no perfect, or right, place to begin. What is important is that you begin. It is beginning in itself that will help you, not beginning at a certain point.

You may argue, "But if I begin by writing about the weather, and what I really want to work on is my relationship with my sister-in-law, how can that possibly help me? I'll be wasting my time!"

A good question, but one you don't need to worry about. In the journal-writing process, if you are working comfortably and honestly and without censor, the issues which are the most important to you will surface eventually. If you practice letting your thoughts flow from your mind to the paper without worrying about whether you are writing the "right" thing; if you don't stop to correct spelling errors or rearrange sentences or change punctuation; if you put your effort into the process, rather than the product; it doesn't matter that you have started by writing about the weather. If you ease up on your conscious writing, and let your unconscious have greater rein, I can almost guarantee that it won't be long before you find yourself writing about your sister-in-law.

If an issue is important to you, it will eventually arise, given the chance. You must give it an outlet first, however. You must get your pen onto the paper and give that issue or feeling a channel through which to flow. Once you start writing about anything, your thoughts and words will eventually take you to the subject matter which is needing expression. But, in order for that to happen, you must first begin to write!

Chapters 10-12 provide a number of exercises for journaling. If you are having trouble finding a place to start writing in your journal, flip through those exercises and find one which appeals to you. It doesn't matter which one you choose. What matters is that you start writing. Put the title of the exercise at the top of your page (See? You've got something on paper already!) and simply begin. If you find yourself switching subjects halfway through the exercise, that's O.K. Don't stop to get back on track, just keep writing. Let whatever comes up come up. You've started!

> *"I always start by writing the date and the weather at the top, because it's benign. The date is the date and the weather is the weather. It takes up part of the page, and then all of a sudden I'm writing!" -Claire*

> *"I'd write down all of my feelings. It would help me to get rid of them and it was like talking to myself instead of harping on and on to someone else." -Lynne*

Common Block 2: "I can't write — I flunked English in school."

If the only experience you have had with writing has been in a formal English class, then it is no wonder you're hesitant, if not downright scared, to pick up a pen. Classes in English instruction serve an important purpose in our educational system. They teach our language; and, they teach it correctly. They teach the rules and the regulations and the what-to-do's and the what-not-to-do's. They teach this information so that the people in our society will be able to communicate with each other in a clear, understandable manner; so that they can speak and write without sounding like infants; and, so that the little third grade girl or boy who will someday grow up to be president or ambassador or Supreme Court judge will not embarrass us in front of other countries by saying things like, "my vice-president and me," or "ain't you got a nice country!" or "sorry, buddy, but you is guilty."

For the purposes of writing in a journal, however, English class is over. If you're worrying about indenting paragraphs, run-on sentences, and transitional phrases, you will not be placing your attention on the matters of journaling importance. The journal does not care if you spell words correctly or capitalize proper names or split infinitives. In your journal, the emphasis is not on the look or sound of the product, but on the process. It doesn't matter how you write as much as that you write.

Your journal is one place that you should forget about the rules, and concentrate instead on the act of writing. Stop editing yourself, and use that energy to get the words flowing from your heart to the blank pages in front of you. Fill those pages! Not with the theme written on the black board, but with what is important to you personally. Remember, no one is going to come after you wielding a bright red marking pen and go through your letters to yourself to cross out extraneous words, point out dangling participles or put a grade at the top for grammar. You're free!

Some of you may find that your writing actually does improve after keeping a journal for some length of time. The more you write for your personal use, the more comfortable you become with the writing process, and sometimes this is enough to improve your writing skills all by itself. Let this be a pleasant side-effect of journal-writing, however, don't let it be a concern.

> *"I like to write in my journal because I can just write sentences that don't make sense. I can write without commas or spelling or write things that don't go together."*
> *-Maggie*

Common Block 3: "As soon as I pick up a pen, my mind goes blank."

"Writer's block," as this experience is usually called, is as common a phenomenon to people who write as the writing itself. A writer can walk around all day, their mind brimming with brilliant ideas just begging for expression, and then as soon as the pen cap comes off, or the computer screen lights up—whammo—the mind blanks out.

It is likely, therefore, that as a journaler, you will have the same experience at some point along the way. Don't let this discourage you in your goal to keep a journal. Writer's block is common; it will probably happen to you more than once; and it is only temporary. It has nothing to do with your ability to be a successful journaler.

There are many reasons that you may develop writer's block. You may be under physical stress, coming down with the flu, or worrying about an upcoming dinner party, graduation, or vacation. You may be over-tired, overworked, or overwrought. You may be experiencing a very strong defense against something that you really should, but don't want to, be writing about. Often you will be able to find a good reason for your block. At other times you will not. Whatever the explanation, it is probably natural, and what you need to do is not worry about it, but make an effort to get past it.

The most frequent suggestion I make in this situation is to simply pick up your pen and begin writing. "But that's just what I can't do!" you say. I know. But, that is only partially true. You may feel like you can't write anything, but what you are really saying is that you can't write anything of importance. Most writer's block kicks in when you are overly concerned about the content of what you are about to put on paper. You aren't sure of the "right" place to begin, or whether the topic is good enough, or simple enough, or interesting enough. You are confused about the direction you are heading, or even if you have any direction at all. Most often you hold some fear about the content of what you are going to write.

In reality, however, you are capable of performing the act of writing. You can physically pick up that pen, put the tip to paper, and move it so as to form a readable message—whether that be a word, a sentence, a paragraph, or a page. You may not be able to come up with something you want to write, but you can write something. And that is all you need to begin.

There is a timed, freewriting assignment which I give to all of my writing students. They are asked to write on any subject continuously, for ten minutes, without stopping at all. The initial reaction to this assignment is, "You've got to be kidding, what would I say?"

Again, the problem lies in what to say. As you have already read, the focus in journal writing is not on the product, but on the process. And for that reason I tell my baffled students, "Write anything. I did not say that you had to write anything good, or even coherent, in this time. I only said that you had to write. If you wish to write, 'This teacher is off her rocker,' for the next ten minutes, fine, you may. Even if you write that, but don't stop writing for ten minutes, you will have succeeded with the assignment."

This idea generally brings a few snickers, but when the ten minutes is up, the students are amazed that after three or four minutes of writing "This teacher is off her rocker," they very naturally and without any great effort, drift right into another, different sentence. That sentence led to another, and that to another, and suddenly the ten minutes were up. And, even those who swore up and down that their minds were completely blank had before them ten minutes worth of thoughts on their paper.

Write, "I hate journaling, it's too hard." Write, "abcdefghijklmnopqrstuvwxyz." Write your name. Write your address. Write something. I had one student who always started out assignments writing children's nursery rhymes. After four or five lines of "Little Jack Horner" or "Mary Had A Little Lamb," she would move into the assigned topic, or her own thoughts, and continue writing without a hitch. Give it a try.

> *"I don't know what my problem is lately—when I get bummed out I can't write in here."* -Erin

> *"Sometimes I sit down to write and I'm just not in the mood for talking to myself."* -Maggie

Common Block 4: "I tried journaling, but I couldn't keep it up."

One of the reasons that people often give up on journal

writing, or sometimes don't even start, is because of the high expectations they place on themselves with regard to output. Many people begin journaling with the idea that they must write something every day. They go along for several days without a problem, but then they get busy, or have nothing to say, and they fall behind in the pre-set schedule. Often one day missed will turn into two or three, and suddenly a week has gone by and they haven't written a thing. Their first thought is, "Well, I've certainly failed at journal writing. I guess I just wasn't cut out for it."

In most tasks that we undertake in life, it is necessary to be regular, consistent, and persistent in order to succeed. The same is true of journaling, but in a much more flexible manner. There can be a great deal less structure in the journaling process for the original goals still to be met.

As I discussed in earlier chapters, the amount of time and frequency of writing that you put into journal writing is strictly up to you. If you write every day, once a week, or just as the need moves you, you are still practicing journaling, and you can still benefit from the results. You alone must dictate the frequency with which you write and the volume that you produce. If you are having trouble keeping up with your original schedule, then you have every right to alter it to better suit your needs. Remember, journaling is a personal project. You are answering to no one but yourself in this job. You alone make the rules, set the goals, and find your own best schedule for "work."

If you find yourself thinking that you're a failure at journal-writing because you're not writing every day, let up on yourself a little bit. You have probably set your expectations too high; you need to rethink your plan. Try for every other day, or once a week, or even once every two weeks to start. You can always change again. The beauty of journal-writing is that it grows with you. As your needs change, your activity can change. There is no one standing over you with a whip or a paycheck forcing you to write.

Of course, it may be that journaling isn't the right activity for you. But, if you are frustrated with yourself for not writing enough, there is a good chance that if you simply relax your expectations a bit you will find that journaling is for you, perhaps on different terms, more suited to your schedule and personal needs.

Maybe there is not a real need for you to write every day. Maybe you would be better off writing at the end of each week, or before any big event, or only when your mother-in-law is staying with you. Maybe those are the only times that you have feelings that you need to "write out." That's O.K.! Remember the points made in Chapter 6—only you can best determine when and how often you need to write, and this schedule may vary again and again over the course of your lifetime.

One of the great benefits of journaling is self-awareness. It is important to use some initial self-awareness to listen to and respect your needs with regard to your journal. If you are not writing as often or as much as you had originally planned, this does not mean that you have failed. It means that you have tried, and now you need to try again, in a way more suited to your personal needs.

> *"My writing schedule is irregular. There is no set time every day, but I probably write a couple of times a week. Sometimes I write no more than a paragraph, and sometimes I may sit for half an hour." -Daniel*

Common Block 5: "I'd like to keep a journal, but I just can't find the time."

Time is a scarce commodity in our world today. We emphasize the need for speed with drive-through restaurants, ten-minute oil changes, and Fax machines. We run from home to work to school to day care, and fit our family and personal time in somewhere in between. We seem to have become almost afraid of free time, filling our spare moments with structured activities and things we "should" be doing.

Because of this way of life, we always have an easy excuse to refuse to do something that we don't want to do. We can always say, "I'm too busy." Or, more tactfully, "Oh, I wish I could, but I have to..." We can use our scarcity of time to protect us from the things we don't like or don't want to do.

In general, the things we don't like to do are those that seem either unimportant to us, or that are stress-producing. Have you ever noticed that there are some things that you can always find time for, no matter how busy you are? They are important to you, or they are relatively easy.

Your journaling activity will also be affected by a scarcity of time and your feelings about the activity itself. If you find yourself saying, "I just can't find a spare moment to write," take a spare moment right now to think about why you have time for other activities, but you don't have time to journal.

It may be that you don't see journal-writing as a priority. There are many other things in your life which are more important to you. If this is the case, no problem. Just don't do it. Journaling isn't for everyone, and maybe it's not for you. Don't try to start a journal because you think you "should." You've got to want to do it for it to be beneficial.

However, before you let yourself accept that answer, ask yourself why you are reading this book. If you are such a busy person, you probably only choose to read those things that are of importance to you. Think about this before you abandon journal-writing completely.

It is also possible that you don't find time to write in your journal because for some reason the activity, or just the thought of the activity, is stress-producing. Take another minute to think about why that might be. Maybe you don't like the idea of exploring the things that are inside of you. Perhaps you think you might not succeed at journal-keeping. Maybe you are uncomfortable with spending this time alone with yourself each day.

If any of these reasons or similar ones come to mind, take some time to look at your comfort factor. Have you found a safe, comfortable place to do your journaling? Have you removed any unnecessarily high expectations regarding the product and volume of your writing? Do you feel secure that your private writing will not be read by anyone else? Are you able to let yourself enjoy the experience of spending some time just on yourself—or does that produce guilt for you?

Try to think—or write—about just what it is that is giving you apprehension about writing in a journal. Listen to your gut level reactions. Become aware of how you really feel about this activity.

People don't have much free time to themselves these days. But, if you really want to keep a journal, you can find the time. In fact, it doesn't actually take all that much time. You could have been writing in your journal in the time that it's taken you to read this section on why you don't have time to write.

> *"My God! How long it's been since I last wrote. I've been stubborn about writing since it takes time (I'm basically lazy and busy) and I kept thinking I can handle my concerns in my head. I guess that's not true right now." -Colleen*

> *"I usually write late at night when everyone's asleep because when I'm deep in thought I don't want to be interrupted. There won't be any phone calls, no one will bother me, and I can just sit and think what I want to say with no interruptions." -Claire*

Common Block 6: "I hate writing."

The difference between this common stumbling block and the others presented so far, is that this block does ultimately let you off the hook. There are some people who simply, and legitimately, really hate writing. They would rather pick up a shovel or a calculator or a stethoscope than write a single word. If they have jobs where writing is required, they still don't do it—they hire secretaries. These are people who, if they want to communicate with friends, pick up a phone instead of a pen. If they had to choose between a grueling, four-hour examination or writing a three page paper, they would start studying for the test.

In other words, there are people who despise writing so much, for whatever reason, that they would never be happy or comfortable or be able to stick to it long enough to get any benefit from writing in a journal.

If you are one of those people, that's O.K.! Don't worry that you'll never write your memoirs or keep a running account of your inner thoughts and feelings. You probably will do some other very wonderful things with your life that are more in tune with your own special talents and skills. Maybe you like to swim or paint or sing or work with machines. That's great. That's O.K. Maybe journaling just isn't the activity for you.

If you are still wanting to increase your self-awareness or help yourself make some changes in your life, you can do that without journaling, too. All you need to do is to explore methods other than writing to accomplish that goal. Maybe you would be better helped by reading a book, talking to a friend or professional counselor, taking an interest test, comparing your thoughts with those of others, or simply making an effort to be honest with yourself. These are all viable alternatives to get to know yourself better without ever coming within a mile of a notebook or pen.

If, however, you think you hate writing because you didn't like English class as a kid, or you think you don't have anything to say, or because it takes so much time, or your mind goes blank when you pick up a pen, or because you don't want to write every day—then maybe you don't really hate writing after all. Maybe you just hate the kinds of writing that you've done so far. Maybe you would like journal-writing, if you gave it a fair chance and kept it flexible and easy enough and tuned into your personal needs so that it wasn't an unpleasant chore. If that's your case, maybe you're not a failure at journal-writing, maybe you've just hit a stumbling block, and you ought to give it a second chance.

"I used to write whenever I felt the need strike, but for a year or so I wrote every day. I wanted to try it and just write something real brief every day and see how I liked it. It was a real good exercise, but I found that if I'm not

inspired, it's harder to write." -Mike

*"If I have the opportunity I'll do my journaling on my computer at work. I type faster than I write so on the computer I can get the feelings down far more accurately."
-Elaine*

PART TWO

Journaling Exercises

INTRODUCTION

In previous chapters I have tried to stress that where you begin in your journal is not as important as *that* you begin. I have also said that you alone should determine the content of your entries, and you should trust yourself implicitly in this judgement—free yourself from external rules and constraints.

From past experience with humans (including myself), however, I know it is likely that you may still worry about how to get started, or, once you are started, may wish some structure and guidance at certain points. Your journal-writing may be progressing nicely, but you could benefit from more extensive exploration of your thoughts and feelings in a particular area, or by seeing things from a different angle. Maybe there is one specific problem that you wish to solve, and you need some concrete guidance in working on it.

There is nothing wrong with using external suggestion or structure as a stepping off point for your writing. In fact, this can help you to climb out of a rut or see things from a new perspective. You may be a person who works better with more guidelines provided, just as some of us prefer lined pages in our journal rather than blank.

In the ideal journaling situation, you would be able to get individual suggestions for writing exercises designed to meet your personal needs and goals. Since that is not possible through a book, however, in Part Two I have provided you with a number of exercises to choose from on your own, including an introduction to using the behavior log. Use these suggestions to get you started along the right track, to explore a detour on your journey, or to help you switch tracks all together.

Chapters 10, 11, and 12 contain the exercises. Chapter 13 provides instructions for keeping a behavior log. Chapter 14 gives suggestions for "reading yourself," or interpreting your work from each exercise.

The exercises themselves have been divided into three phases. Phase I exercises in Chapter 10 are designed first of all to get you writing—about anything, and secondly to get you used to writing about yourself and your own life, ideas, and emotions. Phase II exercises in Chapter 11 are geared to get you digging a little deeper, and to encourage you to explore those parts of yourself which you may too often brush under the rug—your needs. Phase III exercises in Chapter 12 become more detailed, and ask you to use some creativity in helping you discover that person who lies within.

Please, do not feel that you have to complete these exercises in any specific order. Or, that the first exercise you try must be from Phase I (Chapter 10). As you may have guessed, I want you to dictate what it is that you try first, second, or third, and not the set-up of the book. Because you are an individual, and different from everyone else who keeps a journal, your approach to these exercises should also be unique. You must work from your comfort level and your needs, and disregard the order of the exercises except to understand why they have been grouped the way that they have.

I would suggest, if you wish to try one of these exercises in your journal, that you skim through the exercises, and simply begin with the one that seems most appealing to you. Don't worry about where you think you "should" begin. Just pick out the exercise that catches your eye—the one that sounds interesting or fun or like "just what you need." Let your unconscious mind guide you. Trust yourself. Feel free to start with one exercise from Phase III (Chapter 12), then do a couple from Phase II (Chapter 11), and maybe do one from Phase I (Chapter 10) last. Or, skip Phases I and III all together, and do only the ones you like from Phase II. The order does not matter. What's important is: 1) you are writing, and 2) you are comfortable with it. That's all. No grades, remember?

Also, if you should feel cramped or turned off by the thought of doing any kind of structured exercise in your journal, that's O.K., too. Then simply disregard these three chapters and keep on with what you're already doing. Trust your gut. If it feels right, it is right. Use these exercises as you best see fit, and you will achieve the greatest benefit from them.

10 BEGIN AT THE BEGINNING— OR ANYWHERE YOU WISH

EXERCISES: PHASE I: Designed to get you writing—about anything, and to get you used to writing about yourself.

EXERCISE 1: "I remember..."

This exercise is designed to get you writing, as well as to help you to go back in time and into yourself. How far back you go is strictly up to you. There is no right or wrong; just trust your memory and intuition.

The first thing to do is to open your journal to a fresh sheet of paper. At the top of the page, write the words: "I remember..." and then continue by writing about the very first thing that comes to your mind. Don't worry if your subject seems silly or out in left field. Don't make any judgements or censor yourself. Trust your first thoughts.

Your memory can be one that occurred 5, 10, or 50 years ago, or one that happened five weeks, five days, or five minutes ago. It can be a monumental event in your life, or something that you do every day. If your thoughts begin to wander, let them, and simply follow where they lead. Trust yourself.

Try to write in detail and to remember as much as you can

about your subject. Keep writing until you have filled at least a page. (Write more if you wish.) Let your thoughts carry you back, and simply record all that you can about that specific event, place, person, era, etc., on paper.

EXERCISE 2: Timed Writing

Many people are used to writing just a few words at a time—your name on a check, a grocery list, or a name and phone number in your address book. This exercise is designed to help you get used to writing more than that. The easier it is for you to write at length without interruption, the better you will become at getting in touch with the thoughts and feelings that come from deep within you.

For this exercise you will need a timer or an alarm clock. You will be asked to set the clock for a specific length of time, and write from the moment you set the clock until the time is up. You may not rely on a wall clock, because that would force you to look up from your writing every so often. It is important that you learn to write for a length of time without interruption.

I suggest that you begin by setting your timer for five minutes. *What* you write in that time is unimportant. The rule is only that you must not stop writing during the entire five minutes. You may write your name over and over again, or you may write, "I do not like this exercise," over and over again. You may write your grocery list or a story, or the words to a song. You may express your thoughts or feelings on any subject. It doesn't matter *what* you write, but that you write. The object of this exercise is to help you become comfortable with writing for longer and longer periods of time. Don't worry if it takes you a while to get used to it. Eventually you will become comfortable, and you will be able to write about increasingly important things.

When you are able to write for five minutes comfortably, and without looking up or pausing to think or examine your pen nib, practice setting the timer for ten, and then fifteen minutes. You should try to work your way up to one half hour of solid writing.

Remember, the important thing is that you keep writing. Don't take a break to sharpen your pencil or change chairs, or, above all, to "think." Just write!

EXERCISE 3: A.M.—P.M. And Everything In Between

What did you do today? What actions did you take? What reactions did you have? Whom did you meet? Where did you go? What did you avoid? What did you embrace? How did you feel?

Start with the first thing you did when you woke up in the morning, and record every activity of your day. You can do this in any number of ways—by listing, using a time schedule (7:00—wake up, 7:30—breakfast, etc.), or simply in freestyle paragraph form. Use whichever method you like the best.

If the thought of recording every minute detail of your day sounds like a monumental task, begin by just recording the important things and fill in the spaces later. Or, start at the beginning and only write as much as you can fit onto one page. Write about everything—your meals, your clothing, your chores, your outings, your responsibilities, and your leisure.

The point of the exercise is to use your daily life—something you are familiar with—as a stepping stone for self-observation in your writing. You must become comfortable writing about yourself if you are ever to explore the deeper parts of your personality. Writing about what you do will help you get used to this. Observation of your actions is also a first step to looking at who you are.

So, start with that first waking moment, and work your way through your day. (Or, start at 10 a.m. or noon if that is your preference!) Be as specific as you can. Try to fill at least one page.

EXERCISE 4: The Physical You

This exercise uses thoughts about your physical representation—your body parts—as a tool for tapping in to the inner you. As in Exercise 3, you are asked to write about something you are familiar with—this time your physical body—to get you used to writing about yourself. Your writing will depend on self-observation, which is a first step toward self-awareness.

Before you begin, close your eyes for a minute and picture yourself with your mind's eye. What do you look like? Now, choose one part of your body—mouth, toe, stomach, neck, ear, derriere, appendix—to begin writing about. You may choose any part you wish—one that stands out, one that you particularly like, one that you don't like, one that you think is silly, or just the first one that comes to your mind.

You can write anything you like about this body part, but be descriptive and detailed. Write about the function of this body part. What does it do for you? What can you do because of it? What couldn't you do without it? When does it get in the way?

Write about your relationship with this part. How do you feel about it? What do you like about it? What do you dislike about it? Talk to this part. What would you say to it if you had the chance?

Next, write about your body as a whole, as if it were separate from you. Write all of the things you like and don't like about it. Write about how it has served you over the years. Think about a time when your body was injured. Write about how you felt when you were hurt, and how you felt when you healed. Write about all the different feelings you have had toward your body over the years. Were you ever afraid of it? Awed by it? Angry with it? Proud of it?

Write about how your body has changed with time, and how you think it will continue to change. How does this make you feel? Write about these things and anything else that comes to mind with regard to your body.

EXERCISE 5: The People in Your Life

Another way to begin writing about yourself is through writing about other people. Not just anyone you see on the street, but the people in your life—the people who affect you, who you interact with, the people with whom you share relationships.

You may choose anyone at all to write about—someone you are very close to or have known for years, or someone you met only once, but still remember. You may write about the person you have loved the most, hated the most, or feared the most in your life. You may write about anyone who has entered your life at any time, whether that was today, yesterday, or when you were a child.

Briefly describe this person as you remember them, and then write about your reactions to them. What was your first impression of this person? How did you act out this reaction? Did your feelings change or remain the same as you got to know them better? Did the two of you grow closer or further apart? How did your actions reflect this growth or change?

Write about the feelings that this person stirred up within you. Were they negative or positive? Did they remind you of anyone you had ever met before? Did you find this person exciting, dull, warm, or cold? In which way was this person similar to you? In which ways were they very different?

Write as much as you can about this person, focusing especially on the relationship between the two of you. Then write about what you cherished most about this person, and what you disliked the most.

EXERCISE 6: Pros and Cons

This exercise will introduce you to list-making, an effective method for simplifying the decision-making process. Recording information in list form offers the advantage of organizing the facts, eliminating irrelevant material, and putting your situation into concrete form so that you may evaluate and deal with it from a better perspective.

The subject of the list that you make here is going to be yourself. Begin with a blank page in your journal and draw a vertical line down the middle of the page from top to bottom. At the top of the left half of the page, write the symbol for "plus" (+), and at the top of the right half of the page, write the symbol for "minus" (-).

Now, think about yourself, your positive points and your negative points. Write as many positive things about yourself as you can think of on the left half of the page, and write as many negative things about yourself as you can think of on the right half of the page.

Write anything you want, but you must follow one rule: For every negative you record, you must also write a positive, and vice versa. If you can't think of a positive to balance a negative, then you can't write the negative.

Write for as long as you can. List items from the most trivial to the most monumental. Everything counts. For example: (Positive) I am a loyal friend, I make great coffee, I have a beautiful new car. (Negative) I bite my fingernails, I lose things a lot, I am nosy.

Think about every aspect of yourself in this exercise—emotional, physical, and spiritual. Make the list as long as you can, but remember to keep it balanced between positive and negative.

EXERCISE 7: Priorities

In this exercise, you are asked to write about the most important things in your life. Take a minute to think about what you would include in that category. Write down a list of these things in the order that they come to you. "Things" may be people, places, activities, or anything else that you deem valuable. Try to list at least five items.

Now, go back and take a look at that list. Compare each item to the others. Which one of these things is your first priority?

Which is second, third, and so on? Rewrite your list so that the most important item is first, and the least important item is last, with all items in between also ordered according to priority.

When you are satisfied with the order of your list, take the item that you have given highest priority, and write at least a paragraph about it. Then do the same for each of the other items on the list. Write about each item's value to you, its characteristics, and why you chose it to be first, second, third, etc. Write about what your life would be like without this item. How would you cope? What would you replace it with?

When you have finished with your present list, make another one, and repeat the exercise. But this time write as if it were five years earlier. What was the most important thing in your life five years ago? Try to remember your priorities back then. How do they compare to your present day list? What has happened to cause them to change, or to remain the same? For more extensive work, and a "big picture" look at your life, repeat the exercise going back every five years until you reach your birth.

EXERCISE 8: Best Friends

Think about all of the people that you know and interact with on a daily basis. Who among them do you enjoy the most? To whom do you give the most? With whom do you most enjoy spending time? Who fills your needs the most completely? Who do you want to call before anyone else when something big happens in your life? Of all of the people that you know, who among them is your favorite friend?

Write this person's name at the top of your paper, and begin to write about them. Write whatever you want, whatever you feel is important. You can describe this person emotionally, physically, and spiritually.   You can describe their relationship with you, through both the activities that you share and the emotional needs that you fill.

Really think about why this person is your favorite. What specific characteristics do they have that make you pick them as Number 1? Be detailed and honest. Give some thought to your answers.

Write about why this person is important to you and what you would do if they weren't there. Write about how your life would be different without them. Write about why you are important to them. How would they react if you weren't there?

Write about what you like about this person as well as what you don't like. What things would you change about them if you could? What do they like best about you? And what would they like to change? Write about what this person has given to you, and what you have given to them. Write anything else significant about this person. Try to write at least a page.

EXERCISE 9: The Things You Do

Everybody works, and everybody plays. How do you do these things? What choices have you made with regard to the different ways that you spend your life?

Write about your work first. Are you a cashier, nurse, butler, musician, limo driver, undertaker, manager, salesperson, cook, counselor, pilot, homemaker, or accountant? Why did you choose the job that you have now? What do you like best about it? What is the hardest part about it? If there was one part of this job that you could hire someone else to do for you, what would it be? Of all its components, which one would you never want to give up doing yourself?

Think about what would happen if you didn't have to work to make money, or if you had a full time nanny to take care of your children. What would you do with your time then? How would you spend your days? In a completely different way? Or pretty much the same?

Now write about your leisure activities. What is your favorite way to spend a weekend? What is your favorite way to spend a week's vacation? Is your hobby physical or mental? Does it put you behind a desk or out on the road? Write about why you like this hobby so much. How does it fit with your personality? Are people surprised when they find out that you do this? Or does it make sense to them?

Finally, write about something that you have always wanted to do, but never have done. What if someone gave you the opportunity to do it tomorrow? Would you take that chance? If not, what would stop you? How does this activity compare to the way you spend your work and leisure time now?

Now, if you wish, write about the things that you avoid doing, and why.

EXERCISE 10: Places in Your Past

In this exercise you are to write about a place that you have known. It doesn't have to be exotic or significant or beautiful. Any place is fine, as long as you have been there at least once. You may write about the house in which you were born, or about your first kindergarten classroom. You may write about your friend's back yard when you were a little child, or about the first time you saw the Grand Canyon or Niagara Falls or the Louvre museum in Paris. Write about your bedroom, or your cottage, or a store that you were in. Write about whatever place comes to mind.

Try to describe this place in detail. It might help you to close your eyes and picture it again. Look around, what do you remember most vividly? Who was there? What were the colors like? What were the sounds and smells like? What did you see overhead? What did you see below you, and to your left and to your right?

Write about how it felt to be in that place. Try to remember what it was like to be you when you were there, and write about it from that point of view. Think about how this place might be different if you were to go back there, and how you would feel about the changes. Were there any things which you would have liked to be different when you were there? Write about them.

Write about what significance this place held for you when you were there, and what it means to you now. Write about what it would be like to go back.

EXERCISE 11: "I Wish..."

Start this exercise on a clean sheet of paper. At the top of the page write the words, "I wish..."

Finish the sentence with whatever comes into your mind first. It can be a monumental wish, a simple wish, a feasible goal, or an impossible fantasy. Maybe you can easily think of a number of endings to the sentence. That's fine. Write them all down, but then go back and choose one to write about more extensively.

Try to describe your wish in detail. Picture it in all of its glory and write about it in its most wonderful, fanciful, fulfilling state. Write about what this wish means to you, and how you would feel if it came true. Let the little child in you imagine the wonder and glory of that wish, and try to put that little child's feelings and thoughts onto your paper.

Try not to censor yourself in this exercise. Let your wishes be wild and impossible. Don't write only about what you think might really have a chance to happen. Write about whatever is your heart's greatest desire, possible or not. If you wish you could fly, write about it. If you wish you were four years old again, write about it. If you wish you'd get a raise or a new set of teeth or a check in the mail, write it down. Let yourself dream. Anything goes.

Write at least a page on each of your wishes.

EXERCISE 12: "I'm Afraid To..."

Your journal is one place where you should be able to go with your innermost thoughts. That includes all the parts of yourself which you may not usually show to the world. In our society, we cover up many of our fears because of another fear—the fear of appearing weak or foolish. In reality, fears are universal. We all have them. We all live with and deal with them. Sometimes we deal with them better than others.

People deal with their fears in different ways. Some of us choose to adjust to them and some of us let them immobilize us.

Some of us ignore our fears, and some of us make a daily public effort to try and prove that we don't have any. Some of us run from our fears, and some of us fight them. Whatever your relationship is with your fears, your journal is a safe place to explore it. This exercise doesn't ask you to overcome or work through your fears, it only asks you to write about them. It asks you to identify one of them, or more if you wish.

At the top of a new page in your journal, write the words, "I'm afraid to..." Then finish the page by completing the sentence. Write whatever comes to your mind, as long as it is honest. Try hard to think about honesty in this exercise, because the subject of our fears is one in which we frequently try to cover up the truth, even with ourselves. Remember, there is no threat to you in your journal. Let out everything that you need to.

You may write about your fear of flying, or of job hunting, or of having a baby. You may write about your fear of being single, or being married, or getting too close, or being too far away. You may write about your fear of bees or of doctors or of heights. There are no "right" or "wrong" fears. Yours are yours. Just write about them. Be honest. Try to fill at least one page.

11 DIGGING A LITTLE DEEPER—
YOUR NEEDS

EXERCISES: PHASE II: To encourage you to explore those parts of yourself which you may too often brush under the rug.

EXERCISE 1: Things That Haunt Me

This is an exercise with two parts. In the first part, you will make a list. In the second part, you will write more extensively on one item that you choose from your list.

It may help you to begin this exercise by first writing the words, "Things That Haunt Me," at the top of the page. Then, begin your list. You may take the word "haunt" to mean whatever you wish. Don't deliberate over the definition, just write whatever comes to mind.

As you write, try not to think too much about the items you are listing on your paper. Rather, keep the action going and your thoughts flowing to the next item. Dig into your memory and your feelings for the answers to this question. Be honest. Both the seemingly trivial and the more significant items are important. Write down anything and everything that comes to mind. Try to get at least five items on your list. If possible, write for a whole page.

When you feel that your list is as exhaustive as you can make it, go back over what you have written and choose one of the items to write about in detail. Start a new page before you begin. Describe this thing that haunts you. Write about your relationship with it, when it was in your life, if it still is, and if not, how it left.

Write about your feelings toward this item. How have they changed over time? Write with some speculation as to how long you think this will continue to haunt you—another year? Five years? Ten years? All of your life? Next, write about why. Why does this particular item haunt you? What is it that won't let you go? Write about any unfinished business you have with this thing. Then, write about how you might try to work on finishing that business.

EXERCISE 2: Dreams

Most everyone who remembers their nighttime dreams spends some time wondering what they were all about. Our dreams often seem to make no sense. They may be isolated stories or they may carry recurring themes. They may be filled with characters whom we don't know, or they may be about familiar friends and family.

The vivid memory of a dream usually brings with it some unanswered questions: "Why did I dream that?" "What does it mean?" "Why did I dream about a person whom I haven't seen in years?" "Why did I dream about a place that I've never been before?" "Why do I always dream about this same thing?," etc. One way to begin exploring your dreams and their possible meanings is to spend some time writing about them and the feelings that are behind them.

This exercise will be the most effective if it is done as soon as possible after waking. That may be the first thing in the morning, or if you are a restless sleeper, in the middle of the night, while it is still fresh within you.

Write first about all that you can remember of your dream in as much detail as possible. Where were you? Who else was there? What was taking place? How long did it last? What was the main theme? What were the sub-themes? Then, go back and write about the feelings which accompanied each part of the dream. What was the over-all feeling of the dream? How did you feel as each scene evolved? Were you happy, frightened, bewildered, mournful? Did you feel brave or helpless in a dangerous situation? Did you feel loving or cold to the people you were with?

EXERCISE 3: Good-byes

Incidents involving separation and loss occur repeatedly to all of us over the course of a lifetime. We leave our families, our childhood, our neighborhoods, our friends, and our jobs. We lose our children, our neighbors, our co-workers and our parents through growth, relocation, progress, and death. Sometimes good-byes are of our own choosing, and sometimes they are brought about by circumstances beyond our control. In any case, leave-takings stir emotions within us. They usually stick in our memories and our hearts long after the actual act has occurred. Feelings about good-byes and separations are usually deep.

In this exercise, you are asked to write about good-byes, and whatever that brings to mind for you. Write about a leave-taking which occurred in your past, or one that you anticipate in the future. Write about an instance in your life when you had to leave a person or place that you loved, or a time when you were able to end something that you hated. Write about a leaving that you experienced with joy, or one that you fought until the bitter end. You may write about a leaving that came about suddenly, or one that had been anticipated for quite a while.

As you describe the situation around the leaving, try to focus on a description of yourself. How did you feel? What were your actions like? How, if at all, did you prepare for the separation? How long did it take you to adjust after the leave-taking?

Describe what leaving in general means to you. What gut-level reaction does it bring? How do you usually respond? Do you cling to the past and fight progression, or do you cast off the old quickly and jump into the new? Do you avoid leave-takings? Or do you bring them on for yourself?

Write about your happiest or your most painful good-bye, or anything in between. Write about leaving your house in the morning or going off to college. Whatever you choose, be sure to write about yourself in relation to the separation and the loss.

EXERCISE 4: What Do I Look Like?

Most of us look into the mirror every day of our lives. We have a good idea of what we look like when reflected in the flat surface of a two-dimensional glass. This information gives us a pretty accurate picture of how we look on the outside. There are, however, other dimensions to ourselves which we cannot see just by looking in a mirror.

This exercise will ask you to take a look at a different part of yourself and through different means. You will be asked to describe who you are rather than what you look like. You will find that information by observing your personal surroundings.

To do this exercise, you must take yourself and your journal to the one place that best outwardly represents you, to the place which holds the greatest amount of your personal material possessions. This may be a bedroom, a den, a bathroom, a closet, a basement, an attic, a kitchen, a studio, a garage, or an office. It may be a room in your home or away from your home. It may be only a portion of a room. This is the place where you should complete this exercise.

When you are there, find a comfortable place to sit, and look around you. What do you see?   Begin to write about yourself, describing yourself as if you were the objects in the room. Use the words "I am" to help you. Finish the sentence with one particular item, or one physical representation of yourself, that you see. For example, you might write, "I am a dust-free book shelf," "I am a half-empty glass of chocolate milk," "I am a soccer ball," "I am striped wallpaper," or "I am a mug collection from around the world."

Use the words "I am" over and over again until you have filled at least one page. Take in your surroundings and apply them to yourself. Be sure to apply only items which are yours, or your responsibility for being there. Be descriptive; use detail. Write about who you are through what you see.

EXERCISE 5: Highs and Lows—A Graph Of Yourself

We have already discussed how putting your ideas onto paper in paragraph or list form can help you to sort through the information in your head. Another method for organizing facts is with the use of a graph.   This physical representation of

Figure #1   A Graph of Yourself

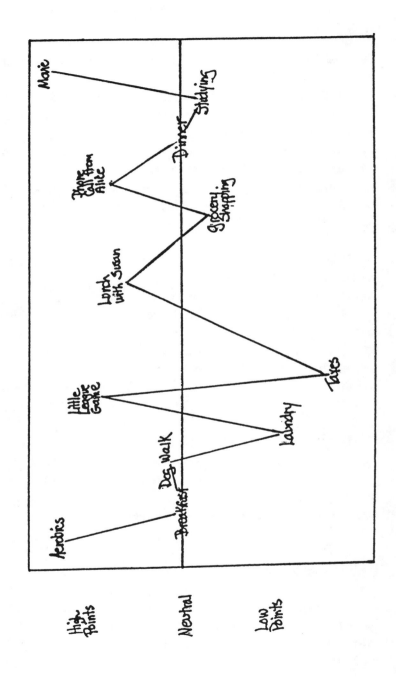

information can help you to see relationships between factors, proportions and statistics more clearly.

Each day you accomplish a great deal of tasks. Some of them you enjoy, some of them you could take or leave, and some of them are downright unpleasant. Making a simple graph of your activities can help you realize your feelings about them more clearly.

Take out a clean sheet of paper, or open your journal to a new page. Draw a line horizontally across the middle of the paper, all the way from the left edge to the right edge. This line will represent neutrality. Everything placed above the line will be considered a "high point," and everything placed below the line will be considered a "low point."

Now, record your day's activities, in the order that they occurred, placing them on either the high side or the low side and at appropriate distances from the center line. For example, if walking your dog today was a pleasant, but otherwise neutral activity, write, "dog walk," just slightly above the center line. If working on your taxes was an especially unpleasant task, place it a good distance below the center line.

When you have finished recording all of the day's events, connect the activities with lines, as shown in Figure 1. You can repeat this exercise using various timetables. Try recording the events of the last year, or a particular season, or of your whole life. Come up with your own timetables, and make as many graphs as you like, observing the patterns which they reveal.

EXERCISE 6: Take A Letter

Writing letters is a method of communicating. In your journal, you can use letter writing to communicate both with yourself and with others. The visible difference between letter writing and regular free form writing is that a letter will begin with a greeting (i.e. "Dear Judy or Tom or Self,") and will end with a salutation ("Love, Jon or Cindy or Me"). The body of the letter will contain information that you wish to express to the receiver of the letter.

A letter in your journal differs from a regular letter in that it may never actually be sent. The purpose of the letter is solely for personal expression. This may be expression that cannot easily, or perhaps should not, be expressed directly to another person. For example, you may write a journal letter to your boss when you feel the need to tell him what an idiot he is and what a monster he is to work for. The purpose of writing the letter is to relieve yourself of the burden of your feelings in a safe manner. Letters such as this serve their purpose through the act of writing them; they should generally not be sent.

Journal letter writing can also be used to rehearse a conversation which you may or may not actually have at a later time. You can write a letter to someone whom you want to meet, but are as yet afraid to approach. You can write a letter to a future employer before a job interview, rehearsing your qualities and marketability. You can write a letter to your father, asking to borrow money. In these cases, writing to a specific person in your journal allows you the chance to practice saying something that may be difficult for you to express verbally.

Letter writing can also be used to explore and clarify feelings and situations for the writer. Writing to yourself helps you to take a step outside of yourself and gain perspective. Writing to another person about your relationship may help you to work through your feelings or see things in a different light before you express yourself directly. Writing in letter form puts you in a position to reveal hidden thoughts and emotions as well as relieve obvious ones.

Choose a person in your life to whom you have something to say, but for whatever reason feel unable to do it in person. Begin your letter with, "Dear_____" and continue from there. Try not to think too much about what you are going to write, but just write it. Let out all of your thoughts and feelings. Remember, this letter does not have to be sent. You will not embarrass yourself or the other person; you will not get in trouble for what you say. Don't worry about organization or clarity or if the other person would understand you. It doesn't matter. What does matter is that you are able to safely express what you have to say.

EXERCISE 7: The Child Within

Although physically each of us age and mature into adults, we never completely leave behind the little child that we once were. No matter how old we get chronologically, emotionally there will always be feelings and thoughts within us that originate from our little child, rather than from our socialized adult selves. There will be times when we will pout, or feel afraid, or wish we could forget all of our responsibilities and be taken care of again. There are times when we will be silly or uninhibited or playful. These are expressions of the child within.

In order to be productive members of society, it is necessary for us to learn to discipline this little child, just as we discipline our own children and as our parents disciplined us. However, it is not healthy for us to suppress the child completely. We need to find appropriate ways to let it have expression.   Laughing, dreaming, and crying at sad movies are a few ways that you can appropriately let your child come out and play. Writing in your journal is another safe outlet. In this exercise, you are asked to sit down with your journal and write not from your usual adult self, but from that little child that is within you.

Think about the people and situations in your life, and write about them from the child's point of view. What does your little child feel about the raise you just received? How does the child feel about your mother's illness? How does the child respond to the news that you will soon be moving out of state? What does the little child want to do when it rains on the day you were planning a picnic?

Repeat this exercise frequently, letting out those thoughts and feelings which you do such a good job of suppressing every day.

EXERCISE 8: A Feeling Log

As has been stressed in the previous chapters of this book, for the benefit of self-expression, as well as self-awareness and self-help, it is important for you to focus on your feelings when you write in your journal. Feelings are a key to your motivation for behavior. To obtain and sustain emotional fitness, it is important to learn to label, accept, and express your feelings in an appropriate manner.

Many people are not used to dealing with feelings in this manner. They are comfortable with thinking and writing about their ideas and their actions, but when it comes to feelings, it seems as if they are traveling in a foreign country: they haven't visited this place before, they don't recognize a thing, and they can't even read the road signs. It can be a very frustrating experience.

To give you some practice in recognizing and labeling your feelings, this exercise asks you to keep a "feeling log," or a running account of the various feelings that you experience throughout the course of a day. You may record your feelings as they occur to you, or you may wish to record them in retrospect, looking back over the whole day or over a particular experience. Whichever method you use, the point is to become aware of the many different feelings that you experience in reaction to the situations and people that you encounter.

If you are not used to taking notice of your changing feelings, you may be aware only of your more intense emotions at first—when you get angry at your sister, when you become confused in a meeting, or when you feel happy about going out for dinner. The more you practice, however, the more sensitive you will become, and your ability to recognize more subtle feelings—such as confusion, melancholy, doubt—will increase. You will find that in the course of any given day your feelings may change hundreds of times.

As you keep track of your emotions, it is important to also record the event or situation that you think stimulated each feeling. The first time you try this exercise, you may only be able to recognize a few, simple feelings. Don't be discouraged; the more you write, the greater your sensitivity will become.

EXERCISE 9: "If I Won The Lottery..."

Everybody likes to dream about what they would do if they won the lottery. We often joke about it with others, and extravagant ideas such as, "I'd quit my job, take a trip around the world, or buy my own country," are tossed about. We usually don't take these speculations too seriously, however, because we know full well that we do have to get up the next morning and go to work, and we do have a week's vacation coming, but we're only going to visit relatives, and we actually wouldn't want the responsibility of running a whole country even if we could afford to buy one. Our thoughts were only part of a pleasant game.

In this exercise, you are asked to think about winning the lottery, but this time in a very serious manner. You are to spend some time thinking very realistically about what would happen if you actually did win a million dollars. Consider all of the realities as you write in your journal: How would you receive this money? In a lump sum, or over a period of time? How much of your winnings would be consumed by taxes? What specific tax forms would you need to declare these winnings? Would you know how to complete them, or would you have to get some help?

What exactly would you do with this money? Write about where it would go, down to the very last dollar. How much would you spend? How quickly would you spend it? What exactly would you buy? Would you spend any on your friends or family? How much? How would you decide what to buy them? Where would you shop?

How about investing? Where would you put your money to make it grow for you? Would you keep your money in something very secure, or would you play the stock market? Or, would you do some of each? How much of each? Would you hire a financial advisor to help you? Would you listen to a friend's advice?

All of these are questions with which you would have to deal if you did win the lottery. Write about how it would feel it make so much money so quickly and with so little effort. Would you be happy, comfortable, nervous? Would you worry about people trying to take advantage of you? How would your life change if this actually did occur? Write in as much detail as you can about exactly how winning one million dollars would affect you.

EXERCISE 10: Some Things Never Change

Whether you are 16, 36, or 60 years old, you have probably been around long enough to get to know yourself and recognize some of the patterns that are present in your life. You are most likely aware of some things that have changed about you over the years, and some things that seem to remain the same no matter what else changes.

In this exercise, you are asked to write about both the changes and the stable factors. Begin by thinking about your inner self, your personality, your values, your needs, and concerns. Look back over your life, and write about those abstract characteristics that changed as you grew and progressed, and those that always remained the same.

You can arrange the information on your paper in a way that will help you see the patterns more clearly (Figure 2). Choose three or four personal traits about yourself, such as: "positive thinker," "workaholic," "procrastinator," and "family-oriented." Write these across the top of your paper. Now, on the left side of the page, going from top to bottom, write today's date, and then the same date five years earlier and then five years before that. Go back as far as you wish. Now make some notes in your columns under the headings that you have chosen. How much did I work five years ago? Was I as family-oriented twenty years ago as I am now? Have I always been such a procrastinator? etc.

Figure #2 Some Things Never Change

	Positive Thinker	Workaholic	Procrastinator	Family-Oriented
June 1 1996	still try + think positively	trying to make ends meet	getting better at responsibility	increased after marriage
June 1 1991	goal-oriented		in college: always put off studying until night before exam	felt distanced from family
June 1 1986	mom always told us to look on the bright side			spent more time with friends than family

Add more and more personal traits as you think of them. Go
back a few more five-year time periods. Or, if you wish, chart
yourself in one-year periods. Shorter time spans will give you a
more detailed view of your growth, while charting in longer spans
helps you to see "the big picture."

EXERCISE 11: Family Tree

Most people have seen a picture of a "family tree," (Figure 3)
even if not their own. Such a picture depicts one's ancestry on
paper in the form of a tree, usually with the subject (you) at the
bottom of the page, and the parents, grandparents, and great-
grandparents, etc. branching out successively above. Siblings and
cousins are included, too.

A picture such as this shows your family configuration, and
makes it easier to see your lineage, your blood relation to other
family members, and your family "statistics". Using this basic
framework along with some additions, you can create a family tree
in your journal which will allow you to see the patterns of personal
characteristics and personality traits in your family, and in turn will
help you to understand some of the factors which affected your
own personality development and your current relationships with
family members.

Try sketching your own family tree in your journal. After all
of the family members are in place, go back and add a list of two
or three descriptive words under each person's name. Choose
words that you feel best describe that relative's personality. For
example: "Mother Olson—warm, jovial, timid." Or,
"Grandfather Jones—towering, worldly, autocratic." Or, "Sister
Kate—intelligent, lonely, attractive."

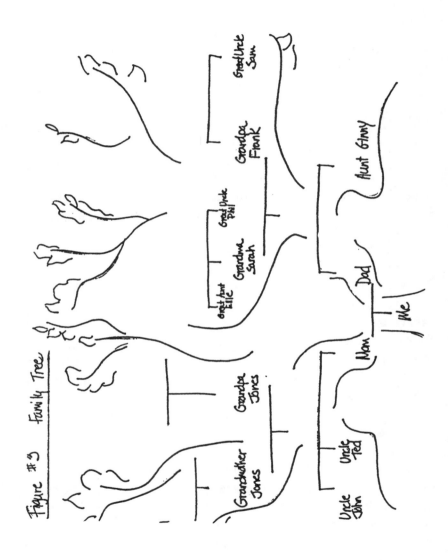

Figure #3   Family Tree

Think carefully about the words you choose. Try to think of those that best identify the person in question. Be as objective as you can. Think about how these people appear to outsiders, as well as to those within the immediate family. You can use words which describe personality traits, or you may wish to use values to describe your relatives. Think about what is important to each of these people: "Mother Olson—family, harmony;" "Grandfather Jones—power, attention;" "Sister Kate—pleasing others, relationships." Give descriptive words for as many relatives as you can. Don't forget to include yourself at the base of the tree.

12 USING SOME CREATIVITY TO DISCOVER THAT PERSON WITHIN

EXERCISES: PHASE III: A more detailed approach asking use of your creativity in helping to discover that person who lies within.

EXERCISE 1: In The Beginning

This exercise will require you to do some traveling back in time. You will be relying on your memory to help you learn about yourself. Find a place where you can relax with your journal, and try to give yourself a good block of time to begin with. You don't have to complete this exercise in one sitting, but you may find that you need a little bit of time to get yourself in gear for the memory work that is asked of you.

Open your notebook to a blank page, get comfortable, relax, and close your eyes. Try to remember as far back as you possibly can, to your very first memory of being alive. To help you set the scene, think about what you know about the town in which you were born, the place where you lived, and the other family members who lived with you. Were there other siblings present at this time? Did you have your own room or were you in a crib in your parents' room? Were both your parents present at your birth? Were both your parents present in your household? You may not have any real memories from the early days and weeks of your life, but you may have been told of the circumstances by your parents or other relatives.   If you know nothing about the beginning of your life, it may help you to ask some questions of relatives who would remember.

As you think about the earliest times in your life, let the memories begin to flow.   You may not be able to remember anything before six years of age, or four, or three.   Most people have some snatches of memory from their preschool years, usually connected to an important or unusual event.   Some, however, draw a complete blank before the age of six or seven.

Once the real memories begin to come back to you, start to write them down.   Write down everything that you can, in as much detail as possible.   If you can, try to write down your feelings from that time in your life.   What was it like for you to be a little child?   Do you get a positive or negative sense of your first few years?   Continue to write down everything you can remember. The scenes will probably be disjointed and far between for awhile. As you follow your growth, you will remember events more completely and accurately.

You can spend a great deal of time on this exercise.   Don't feel that you have to complete it in a few sittings, or in a certain amount of time.   Work on it little by little, for as long as it fulfills your needs.

EXERCISE 2: A Present To Yourself

Pats on the back are too often things that we learn to give to other people, but not to ourselves.   When this is the case, it means that we must rely only on sources outside of ourselves for any positive feedback that we receive.   We have to count on others to keep us feeling good about ourselves, to keep our egos boosted and our self-esteem at a healthy level.

It is important to let people you care about know that they are loved and appreciated. It is a boost for them, and also for you when you receive praise in return. But it is just as important, if not more so, to learn to give positive strokes to yourself. Patting yourself on the back when you deserve it does not have to imply conceit or egoism. Healthy self-esteem consists of an appreciation of your own achievements and qualities as well as a critical eye kept on the areas in which you need improvement. (Maybe if we were better at nurturing ourselves with a kind word now and then, we would have less need to nurture ourselves with excess drinking, overeating, and other material "prizes".)

In this exercise you are to write a letter in your journal. This letter is to someone whom you probably never have written to before—yourself. You should think of it as a love letter of sorts. Not a love letter that you would send to someone you are romantically involved with, but a letter to someone whom you care very much about—a letter to a very close friend.

Being your letter with, "Dear_____," (fill in your own name). In the letter, tell yourself all of the things that you like about yourself, from the smallest to the most important. Be sure to mention any special talents or skills that you have. (Talents include the art of conversation, friendliness, and compatibility, as well as those that we more traditionally think of such as painting, singing, or running a business.) Write about all of the positive traits that you possess. Remember to write as if you were expressing yourself to your best friend.

EXERCISE 3: Point Of View

One of the most valuable skills that you may learn through journal-writing is the art of perspective and objectivity. As discussed earlier, the ability to "take a step outside yourself" is an important step toward gaining true self-awareness. It is also a valuable quality to possess when dealing with other people. Both your personal and professional relationships can only be enhanced by your ability to see the other person's point of view.

You can begin increasing your point of view skills by writing about a particular subject not just once, but twice. First write about a situation, person, or event as you see it through your own eyes. Describe this thing physically and emotionally, and detail your feelings about it. When you feel that you have expressed your opinion as fully as you can, take out a fresh sheet of paper and begin to write about the same subject again, but this time from a different point of view.

To help you get "out of yourself" enough to see things through someone else's eyes, you may have to do a little role-playing. Choose a particular person whom you wish to write "from", and then do your best to think about what it would be like to actually be that person. Close your eyes and picture yourself inside of their body, living in their house with their family, and feeling their feelings. You must get inside of their skin and their experience of the world to be able to see things from their perspective.

Now, begin writing about your original subject, but write as if you were that other person. How would they describe the situation, physically and emotionally? What would their feelings be about it?

The more you practice this exercise, the easier it will become, because you will increase your ability to see things from another point of view. When you feel confident in this area, take the next challenge and use yourself as the subject of your work. Write about how you would be described by your mother, best friend, a stranger, etc. Be as honest as you can.

EXERCISE 4: Dialogue

Most people think of dialogue as the spoken words in a story or script. But you don't have to be an actor or writer to work with dialogue. We all take part in dialogue whenever we have a conversation. Writing in dialogue form is not limited to professionals either. If you can talk, you can write dialogue. And, in your journal you can use that dialogue to learn about yourself.

For this exercise, choose any two (or more) parties to be used as the speakers in a dialogue. From there, you will simply let these characters speak, and record what they say to each other. Remember, this is your journal, not an English class, so you needn't worry about using quotation marks, commas, or "he saids" and "she saids". Concentrate on the process, rather than the product, of your writing.

"But how do I know what these characters will say?" you may be thinking. The answer is that you probably will not know until they begin to speak. Start them off with saying, "hi," to each other if you don't know where else to begin. Then see what comes from there. Or, pick a particular subject for them to talk about. Don't plan what they will say, just begin writing and see what comes out.

Most often, you will want to use yourself as one of the

characters in your dialogue. This is how you will learn about the feelings you have about the other speaker or the topic you are discussing. But there may also be times when you are not a member of the action. Perhaps you want to write a dialogue between your father and your sister, or your head and your heart, or two of your co-workers. That's fine, too. The sky is the limit in choosing your characters.

In fact, your journal affords you the opportunity to use your imagination and create things which are not possible in real life. In reality, if you talk to your work bench, or your stomach, or your goldfish, you will not receive an answer. But in your journal their speaking is not only possible, but necessary. You may find that writing a dialogue with your work station or body parts or pets is more enlightening than silly.

Don't worry about setting scenes or describing situations when you write in dialogue. Just pick your speakers and start writing. See what they have to say to each other. It may be slow-going at first, but soon your speakers will be talking faster than you can write. Let the conversation flow between them. Don't stop to censor or make corrections, just sit back and listen to what they (you) have to say.

EXERCISE 5: This Is How I Look Today

The written word is used most often for journal-keeping, but it is not the only method of recording. Drawing, or self-expression through pictures, is just as valid a mode and can offer new insight as well as a break from your usual writing.

Don't let the word, "draw," scare you! You don't need any artistic skills to be able to successfully complete and benefit from this exercise. What you do need, and the skills that will grow from this exercise, are the ability to listen to your inner self and to see yourself from the *inside out*, instead of the other way around.

You may use the same materials for this exercise that you always use for journaling, or you may choose to use materials more conducive to drawing. It doesn't matter what you use, as long as you are comfortable. Remember, you are not in an art class, and your drawing will not be graded, or even seen by another person. So don't be shy, just draw.

The subject of your drawing is going to be yourself. You are to draw a picture of yourself, but in a different manner than you are used to seeing. You are not to draw yourself as you look on the outside, but by how you feel on the inside.

Take out a blank sheet of paper, and at the top of the page write, "This is me today." Now begin drawing yourself according to how you feel. Are you feeling tired? You may want to draw your eyes closed. Are you excited? You may put a big grin on your face. Are you feeling generous? You may want to draw yourself with a big heart. Are you feeling strong today, or weak? How would you depict this? Do you feel like talking to other people, or making yourself very small and sitting in a corner? How would you draw this?

Ask yourself these kinds of questions as you draw your picture. Don't feel bound to stick with conventional art forms. I once had a student who drew herself as a maze. Her picture didn't look anything like a human being, but it was right on target with how she was feeling that day. Draw yourself as you feel, not as you think you look. After you have completed your picture, go back and look at each body part that you have drawn. Label each part on your paper, and write a brief explanation of why you drew it the way that you did.

EXERCISE 6: Family Portrait

This is another exercise which asks you to draw instead of write. Once again, artistic ability is unnecessary. Don't let the word, "portrait", bother you. What you will actually be drawing is a bunch of circles and lines. (No problem!)

To begin this exercise, find a fresh page in your journal and draw a large circle or rectangle around the perimeter of the page. This will be the frame of your family portrait. You may make it look more like a frame by giving it a double edge.

The next step is to begin drawing the members of your family within the framed area. You may draw their full bodies, or only their faces. You may draw with great detail, or with very little detail. You may put whatever people that you want to include into the picture, whether that be only the members of your immediate family, or including your in-laws, your second cousins, your great-grandparents, or whomever. There is no right or wrong way to draw this picture. What is important is that you draw from your gut.

As a second version of this exercise, take a new page, make another frame, and this time draw a picture of your friends instead of your family. These may be your friends from work, from the neighborhood, from school, from your club, or whatever combination of those groups that you choose. Do what feels right for you. Try to draw from your heart rather than your head. Draw from your feelings.

EXERCISE 7: The Editor

Have you ever heard anyone say, "If I only had the chance to live that over again, I'd do it very differently?" Some things that happen to us we are very pleased with, and some things we are not pleased with. Some things in life we have great control over; some things we have little or no control over. Did you ever wish that your life were a story, and you could edit it just as you pleased? You could take out the parts that you didn't like, and lengthen the parts that you loved. Or, you could write in the good times over and over again, and you could leave out the sad times altogether.

In your journal, it is possible to be that editor. Begin this exercise by thinking of a nightmare that you have had. (If you don't remember your night dreams, choose something that you are conscious of being afraid of during the day.) Now, write about the nightmare in as much detail as possible. After you have recorded everything you can remember, go back to the parts that frighten you or that you don't like, and use your pen or pencil to blacken them out. Go over the words again and again until you can no longer see them.

Now, start a new sheet of paper, and rewrite the dream in a more pleasant way. Write it the way that you wish you had dreamed it the first time. Turn the bad parts into good parts. Turn that nightmare into a pleasant experience. Go ahead—you're the editor. You have the power. You are in control.

After you have edited your dream, do the same thing with a real scene from your life. Is there something you wish you could do differently? Something that always ends in a way that you don't like? Something you wish you could change? First write your story the way it really is, then go back and blacken out the parts that you don't like. Finally, rewrite the story the way you would prefer it to be. Remember, the control is in your hands.

EXERCISE 8: On Your Own

You may be an adult—a voter, a parent, or an employer. You may have children of your own, be financially secure, and be an upstanding citizen of your community. You may be in charge of running a household, paying a mortgage, and making important decisions that affect other people's lives. It may be that many years have passed since the time you lived under your parents' roof and by their rules.

Although there is distance between your life now and your life as a minor, you are still, and always will be, a son or daughter. And, as is the case with many, you may still find yourself making decisions influenced by that fact.

This situation in itself is normal. We are all influenced by our upbringing and by the people responsible for it. Some of us choose our life's work because of our parents' influence, and we are very happy. Some of us choose our ideals and values because of what our parents taught us, and take pride in them. Some of us raise our own children the way we were raised, because we felt it was a good way.

There are others of us, however, who have problems dealing with our parents' influence. We may have trouble completely separating from them and developing our individuality. We may feel smothered by our parents, even though they live many miles away. We may feel that we can never make a decision on our own because we are always wondering about our parents' reaction. This exercise will teach you something about your present connection to your parents, whether it be healthy or problematic.

Use your license of imagination and pretend that our space program is a little more advanced than it actually is. Pretend that it is not only possible, but common, for people to live on Mars. *Pretend that your parents have decided to move there.*

Now, write about this. What is your gut reaction to their announcement? How will this affect you? It may help to write at the top of your paper, "If my parents moved to Mars, I would..." Then complete the page. Think about how you would react to this news. How would you feel? What would you do? In what ways, if any, would your life change after they had gone? Write about your behaviors, but remember to look for the feelings behind them, too. Focus your writing on those feelings.

EXERCISE 9: "If I Were..."

Your journaling license for fantasy allows you to reach beyond your reality in this exercise and explore yourself from yet another perspective. You will need to cast off all of your learned constraints and conventions and trust your imagination. Try not to think, "impossible," or "silly," but to use the exercise as a step toward increasing self-awareness and knowledge.

At the top of your paper write the words, "If I were an animal, I would be a..." And then complete the sentence. (Don't stop at a one word answer, of course.) Consider this question from two different views. First, think about what animal your personality would make you. Answer the question, "why?" Think about your personal characteristics. What is it specifically about you that would connect you with this animal rather than any other?

Next, write about the animal that you would like to be if you had the choice. (And, why?) What characteristics about this animal appeal to you? How would it feel to be this animal? Think about details. Would you be a rabbit, lion, frog, deer, dove, eagle, snake, puppy, fox, leopard? Would you fly, swim, run, or crawl? Where would you live? Would you rather be a wild animal or someone's pet?

After you have completed this question, turn to a clean page and write, "If I were a food, I would be..." across the top. Answer this question in the same two parts as you did the first: what would your personality make you, and then what would you prefer to be? Again, think about details. Would you be spicy? Sweet? Bitter? Would you be served hot? Cold? Frozen? Would you be an entree or a side dish? A bread or a dessert? A meat or vegetable? What are your ingredients? What would you be garnished with?

Give some thought to this exercise. Try to write at least a page on each question.

EXERCISE 10: Role Models

We all are who we are today due in part to the influence of "role models." Role models are the people whom we were exposed to, and whom we watched and imitated when we were little children. These people, either purposely or through association, taught us how to perform the particular roles that we would take in our lives. We learned a great deal about how to be a woman, man, parent, employee, aunt, friend, salesperson, fire-fighter, teacher, mechanic, etc. from the people we first observed in those roles. Our role models played a part in the way we live our lives today.

Parents and older family members are the most common role models, but we were influenced by others, too: celebrities, characters in literature, neighbors, babysitters, coaches, counselors, etc. In this exercise, you are asked to think about the specific role models that were present in your life. Who were the people in your early years who taught you how to act in the world? Who were the people who taught you what to say, what not to say, what to be afraid of, what to embrace, what to strive for, and what to avoid in life?

Think of specific people from your youth, and write about them. In what ways did they influence you? How did they affect who you are and the things you do today? Why were these particular people your role models and not others?

As a variation, write about the heroes in your life today. A hero is someone whom you specifically choose to idealize or emulate. Think about your heroes. Are they similar or different from your early role models? Are they similar or different from you? What traits do they have that you admire or respect? Write about your heroes in the same detail that you gave your role models.

EXERCISE 11: Never Say Never

There are some situations in life about which we think we can honestly say, "That would never happen to me!" There are some things we avoid because they are just "not us". By the time we are adults, we think that we know ourselves well enough to make some predictions about how our lives will unfold, the things that are likely to happen to us, and those which could "never" happen.

In this exercise, you are going to address one or two of those things that would "never" happen to you. Take a minute to think about it if you like, and then choose a situation to write about in detail.   Begin by examining the situation and listing the characteristics that make it so unlikely. Think about why this might happen to someone else, but not to you.   What characteristics of your personality would repel this situation?

Try to write at least a page on the first question, and then take the exercise one step further. This time write about what would happen if this thing actually did occur. Don't worry about the fact that you are convinced it never will happen; you may very well be right. But stretch your imagination and consider the consequences if somehow the impossible did occur.

What would happen to you? How would you feel? What actions would you take? What course of events would follow? How would you handle the situation? What resources would you use to get through it?

You may find it initially difficult to think about this situation because it seems so far from reality. But give it some time. Try to give the situation some real thought. Do your best to address it in your journal.

EXERCISE 12: Looking Ahead

People love to ask children what they want to be when they grow up. And, kids are usually pretty good daydreamers with regard to the future. Most of them are still innocent to struggle and failure, and wide open to possibility.

This exercise will ask you to put away your knowledge of adulthood and reality for awhile, and try to recapture the optimism of your youth. You are going to write about the future. Not the real future, but an ideal future. A future where anything and everything is possible—and anything and everything that you want is yours.

Pretend that the calendar has just been moved ahead five years. You are still yourself, but five years have passed, and, you are living out your ideal day.   Forget your budget, forget responsibilities.   Pretend that you have just woken up in the morning. What will happen to you on your ideal day?

Begin by writing about where you are.   Describe your surroundings.   Are you alone?   Are there others in your household? Where are you living? What is the very first thing that you do upon awakening?

Continue writing by following yourself through the entire day. Describe everything through "ideal" glasses.   Your activities, surroundings, and relationships are all what you would choose if your ideal day could really happen. Think about the people in your life, the way you would spend your time, the choices you would make. What would you like to be wearing, eating, working at? Who would you want to be with you?

Remember, you have no constraints except your own imagination and desires. The sky is the limit. What is it that you would want?

EXERCISE 13: Decisions, Decisions

Every day of our lives, we make hundreds of decisions. Some of them are so automatic we don't even realize that there is choice involved. Some things we assume so readily, we feel that we don't really have a choice at all. Will you choose to get up in the morning or stay in bed? Will you get dressed? Will you brush your teeth? Will you drive your car to work or walk? Will you eat three meals or one?

In fact, we do have alternatives in almost every decision that we make. The choices may be limited or wide, the decisions may be big or inconsequential, but they are there nonetheless. For each decision that we make, a choice is made. In this exercise you are asked to do some exploration of the reasons behind those choices.

Begin by listing in your journal some of the biggest decisions that you have made in your life. These may include the decision to take or change a job, to marry, have a child, move away, spend a large sum of money, give something up, start something new, etc. Then, go through that list of decisions and write about each of them in more depth. Think about what it was that motivated you to make each decision. What influenced you? What caused you to first consider this move, and then ultimately to take action? What were you avoiding, or what were you moving towards?

Don't assume that you did everything because you "had to," or because that's "just the way you do things." Examine the reasons behind your actions, and the feelings that are connected to those actions. Write about them.

13 THE BEHAVIOR LOG
A Way to Monitor Behavior Patterns

Up to this point, I have tried to stress the importance of structuring your journal-writing experience to fit your personal needs. I have advocated flexibility, the "no rules" theory, and the idea that your journal should be a place where you are free to express yourself in your own way and your own time.

With the use of a behavior log, these guidelines change dramatically. A behavior log is a highly-structured journaling technique designed to be used with a specific goal in mind and specific rules to follow. The more closely you follow the rules, the more effective the exercise will be. If you ignore the rules completely, there will be little or no benefit gained from keeping the log.

The behavior log is used to monitor behavior patterns. Its ultimate goal is to help you understand why you are doing what you do, and, if this behavior is negative, to help you to change or eliminate it by finding alternative ways to fill your needs. Recording information in a log helps you to become aware of the specific characteristics of your actions (self-awareness), and to interrupt the unwanted behavior (self-help).

Any type of behavior can be monitored in a log. You may wish to keep track of a positive behavior—one that is pleasant or beneficial to you, or you may wish to record a negative behavior—one that is unpleasant or problematic. The log is most

Figure #4 Behavior Log

DAY	TIME	PLACE	THOUGHTS PRIOR TO ACTION	FEELINGS PRIOR TO ACTION	ACTION (What I did)	ALTERNATIVE ACTION (What I could have done)

often used to deal with negative behavior patterns, but examples of both will be given here.

Figure 4 shows an example of an as yet uncompleted behavior log. You can see that there is space for the writer to keep track of various facts about the behavior that is being monitored. Please note my stress on the word, "facts". Many of the exercises in this book have encouraged you to be creative, and to use your imagination to its fullest. In a behavior log, however, there is no room for fiction. Hard, cold facts are what you are looking for.

The basic rules for keeping a behavior log are as follows:

1.) Choose a specific behavior that you wish to monitor.

2.) Each time you find yourself about to perform this behavior, stop and fill out your log.

3.) Be sure to fill in each column. (If you are monitoring a negative behavior, it is most important to record the thoughts and feelings that you experience prior to the action, and an alternative behavior to the negative one.)

The log should be carefully filled out, and also carefully examined later. By keeping track of the thoughts and feelings connected to your behavior, you can begin to understand what it is that triggers your actions. The detailed recording of time, place, and day increases your awareness of your behavior patterns. As you can guess, the more immediate and the more honest the recording of facts, the more effective the behavior log will be.

The log in Figure 5 shows three examples of negative behavior monitoring. These three behaviors have been recorded in one log for the sake of conserving space. Were you to monitor three

Figure #5 Behavior Log

DAY	TIME	PLACE	THOUGHTS PRIOR TO ACTION	FEELINGS PRIOR TO ACTION	ACTION (What I did)	ALTERNATIVE ACTION (What I could have done)
Sun.	8pm	Home	Thinking about the presentation I have to give at the PTA board meeting tomorrow	Nervous!	Ate a pint of ice cream	Could have called Sue & talked to her about it
Tues.	1pm	Work	I'm doing all the work on this project! It's not fair; I'm always the one who puts out more effort - and I'm the one who's got the most responsibilities at home, too!	TENSION. Feel like I want to scream, or explode, or punch something.	Blew up at co-worker. Said things I didn't mean	Maybe I should have taken a break. I did work through lunch; that didn't help matters. I could have gotten out of the office for awhile.
Fri.	5pm	Mall	Nothing seems to be going right these days. Everyone else gets all the breaks.	Feeling sorry for myself.	Spent $250 on 2 new dresses that I don't need + can't afford	Could have bought a less expensive item, like earrings; could have pampered myself with as long as not both as home (while making a list of all the things that are right in my life!)

different behaviors of your own, you would use a separate logging form for each one. (For your own sake, and the insurance of your success, I would not recommend trying to work on more than one behavior at a time.)

Please note that the goal of using a behavior log is to fill out the log before you perform the negative behavior, thus using your awareness and the interruption in your action to keep you from ever performing the act. However, you may not be able to do this right away. In each of these examples, the recorder filled out the "Action" column first. They performed the negative activity before they took time to think about it.

This is how many behavior patterns get started in the first place: An action takes place once and fulfills a need, it is repeated, fulfills the need again, is repeated again, works again, and soon becomes a habit. Once action becomes habit, we tend to repeat it without giving it much, if any, thought. Since it is initially hard to break a time-worn habit, many people find that they begin their logging after the action has occurred.

If this is your situation, don't be discouraged. Remember, your goal is to log before you act, but it may take some time and effort to reach that goal. Many of you are fighting ingrained habits that took you years to build up. It will also take some time to break them down. What is important initially is that you become aware of the circumstances surrounding your actions. Next, you want to become aware of the thoughts and feelings that trigger those actions. After that you will need to think about alternative actions that can fulfill your needs in a healthier manner. And finally, you will learn to perform those alternative actions instead of the negative behavior.

Self-awareness comes before self-help. Be gentle with

yourself. You are striving toward an important goal. Assume that you will make mistakes, but don't let them keep you from taking another step. Eventually, your efforts will pay off.

As I said earlier, you may also use a behavior log to monitor positive behaviors. Perhaps you wish that you could be more patient with your children. To increase this activity, you can use your behavior log to help you become aware of what makes you patient now. You can begin by recording specific times when you do exhibit patience (under "Action", since being patient is the action you wish to monitor). You may find that you are most patient on days when you have exercised, or on days you have talked to a particular friend, or on days after you've gone to bed an hour earlier. Awareness of these patterns can suggest that you might increase your patience by increasing these other actions. Maybe you should try to exercise several times a week instead of just once. Or give that friend a call when you feel stressed. Or make it a point of getting a good night's rest every day. (These things may be easier said than done, but remember, you do have choices about your priorities. See what you can do. Even a small change can help.)

Once in awhile, just the accurate writing in a behavior log will cause a change in your behavior. But, this is usually not the case. A behavior log will not automatically "work" after a certain length of time. More often, change will require some additional effort on your part. The behavior log can increase your self-awareness by pointing out your patterns of thought, feeling, and action. But it is up to you to use that information to make your own changes. You must take the steps to work with your new self-awareness in making the changes which constitute self-help.

14 INTERPRETATIONS
Guidelines for interpreting each exercise in Chapters 10, 11, and 12

Completion of any of the exercises in this chapter will give you some practice in focused journal-writing, as well as provide some insight as to who you are, and why you are that particular person. Reading over your writings with an open and inquiring mind, and using the guidelines for "reading yourself" in Chapters 8 and 9, will allow you to gain additional insight and add to your growing self-awareness.

To offer further assistance in learning from your work, I am providing specific interpretive guidelines in connection with each exercise. You should use these guidelines to stimulate your thinking about yourself, your behaviors, and your motivations. This is by no means an exhaustive interpretation. Hopefully, the suggestions will serve as a springboard for your own further thinking and questioning about the characteristics of the inner you, and how they came to be.

(To keep your responses as fresh and honest as possible, it will be most helpful to complete each exercise before reading over its guidelines for interpretation.)

INTERPRETATIONS: PHASE I (Chapter 10)

EXERCISE 1: "I Remember..."

No matter what your age or background, you have literally hundreds of thousands of experiences in your past. You began making memories the day you were born, and you have continued ceaselessly. Each day you add new memories to your portfolio. With that thought in mind, the most important observation to make with regard to this exercise is the significance of the memory that you chose to write about.

Think about the fact that out of all those hundreds of thousands of memories, you chose, whether consciously or not, this one particular memory about which to write. Ask yourself why. What is it about this memory that is significant? Why did it come to you now?

You may want to think about what is currently happening in your life that connects with your memory in any way. Explore this from a factual as well as a feeling point of view. Write your thoughts and interpretations in your journal.

EXERCISE 2: Timed Writing

How easy or difficult was it for you to begin this exercise? Did you start by writing the same sentence over and over? Did you eventually get into a specific subject? (If you spent the entire time copying the alphabet, don't be discouraged, but ask yourself why? What are you resisting? Keep trying the exercise until you break through this.)

Next, think about how easy it was for you to write for the entire length of time. Did the time seem to go quickly or slowly? What defenses did you use to keep yourself from writing—did you look at the clock, stop to reread your writing, erase or make corrections, think about what you were going to write instead of write?

Because there was no specific content assigned to this exercise, another point of interpretation will be what you did choose to write about. Ask yourself why, out of anything you could have picked, did you choose the particular topic you did. And, did you stick to the same subject for the entire time, or did your thoughts wander? If you changed subjects midstream, find the exact point where your topic changed, and ask yourself why. Look for patterns. Do you always seem to change the subject when you get into a certain area?

Think about your answers to these questions. How do they jibe with the way you think about yourself? Does this sound typical of you? Do these patterns mesh with the patterns in the rest of your life?

EXERCISE 3: A.M.—P.M. And Everything In Between

Read over your recorded day as if you were reading about a stranger. Just by reading about how this person spends their time, what impressions do you get? What do you learn about this person? What are their priorities? What can you tell about their personality? What are their values? Their morals? Their qualities? Their weaknesses?

Now take an overview of your day from your own point of view. Is this the way you like to spend your time? How much control do you have? As much as you'd like? What feelings do you experience as you read over your writing—satisfied? discouraged? How can you make changes to spend your time in a manner more of your choosing? Or, how can you insure that you continue the patterns that you like?

Take a little time to think about your feelings as you did the exercise. What did it feel like to write about yourself? Were you comfortable? How closely did you keep to writing just about yourself? Did you trail off onto tangents about other people or other things? Are you used to spending time on yourself? Why or why not?

EXERCISE 4: The Physical You

Of all the body parts that you own, which did you choose to write about in the first part of the exercise? Ask yourself why. Is this a part that you have thought about a lot in the past? Do you have a history of peace or conflict with this part? Think about the parts that you didn't choose. Were there some you avoided on purpose? Why did you avoid them? What feelings do they stir within you?

Is thinking about your physical self something that you are familiar with? Or do you rarely think about your body? Is it easier or harder to write about your physical self than your inner self? Why? What specific feelings did you experience as you wrote about your body? What specific feelings do you get as you read back over your writing?

Think about your body image as compared to your self-image. How closely are they related? Does your self-worth depend more on your body image or on the way you feel about your inner qualities?

EXERCISE 5:   The People In Your Life

Was it difficult or relatively easy to choose a person to write about for this assignment? Why did you choose the person that you did? What significance do they hold for you? Why did you choose to write about a close friend rather than a casual acquaintance (or vice versa?) Is it easier for you to write about yourself, or another person—and why?

If the person you wrote about is someone close to you, read back over your description of them, and think about what having a person like this in your life tells you about yourself. Likewise, if you wrote about someone you dislike, what does disliking this kind of a person tell you about yourself?

Do you see patterns in the kinds of people whom you choose to bring into your life? Are you satisfied with these patterns, or would you like to make some changes in them? Are these the same type of people who were in your life five years ago? Ten years ago? How do the changes, if any, reflect the changes in your self?

EXERCISE 6:   Pros And Cons

Which was it easier for you to come up with—positive qualities about yourself, or negative traits? Think about the reasons for your answer. Who or what influenced the way that you think about yourself today? How did you learn to look at yourself in a negative or positive light? Is this pattern the same or different from the feedback that you were given as a child? If it is the same, are you pleased with your attitude? If it is different, why and how did it change? Think about the roots of your self-concept.

Now, look at your lists more closely. Which are there more of—emotional, physical, or spiritual characteristics? Which are there more of in the positive category? In the negative category? What does this tell you about the way that you think about yourself?

How does the way you look at yourself coincide with the way you look at the rest of the world? Are you more negative or positive about one or the other? Think about why.

EXERCISE 7: Priorities

Look at the list of priorities that you have made. Pretend that this is not your list, but one that you found somewhere. Read the list from this objective frame of mind, as if you do not know who wrote it. What kind of a picture do you form about the writer? What does this list of priorities tell you about them? What kind of a person are they? Would you like to become friends with them?

Now step back into your own perspective and read your list again. What do these priorities deal with? Are they money-oriented? Family or relationship-oriented? Self-oriented? Other-oriented? Physically or spiritually oriented? What does this tell you about yourself?

Look back at how your priorities have or have not changed over the years. What do these changes say about the course of your life?

EXERCISE 8:   Best Friends

Read over your description of this person as if you didn't know them. What kind of a person would you expect to be this person's best friend? Is that anything like yourself? Would a stranger think it sensible or odd that the two of you are good friends? Why?

What does having this person as a best friend tell you about yourself? What does it tell you about your interests? Your values? Your priorities?

Think about what you have written. Were some parts easier or harder to write than others? Are there any parts of the exercise that you skipped, or things that you didn't want to write about this person? Ask yourself why, and how does this connect to who you are?

How did you see yourself surviving without this person? What does your need for a relationship with them tell you about yourself? Could you foster their qualities within yourself if you needed to?

EXERCISE 9:   The Things You Do

Look back over your exercise and make a general list of everything that you do with your time. Now make some observations about the activities on that list. Which of these activities have you chosen because you want to do them? Which of these things do you do because someone else told you that you "should" do them? Do you do more things that you want to do, or that someone else told you you should do? Does the proportion seem healthy to you?

Do you see patterns in the things that you either like or don't like to do? What do these patterns tell you about yourself? Think about where your preferences first originated. Why do you think you like the hobby that you have rather than another?

As you read over this exercise and answer the above questions, try to be aware of the feelings which are stirred within you. Be sensitive to your physical and emotional responses to each of the questions. What do you learn about yourself by listening to your feelings?

EXERCISE 10: Places In Your Past

Just as you have many memories and know many people, you have also visited many different places over the course of your lifetime, even if you have never left your home town. If you have not visited Istanbul, Saudi Arabia, or Stockholm, you have still been to a library, a movie theater, a grocery store, a restaurant or a park. There were many places for you to choose from to do this exercise. Why did you choose the one that you did? What does this tell you about yourself right now?

What kind of feelings do you have connected to this place? Did you choose it because it was safe? Or scary? Does it give you a feeling of agitation? Or peace? What is going on in your life right now that is connected to this place or your feelings about it in any way?

If this was a positive place, think of ways that you can recreate its atmosphere in your life today. If it was a negative place, think of ways you can eliminate its characteristics in your life.

EXERCISE 11: "I Wish..."

Think first about the wish that you chose. What are the qualities behind that wish that you are really talking about? (For example, if you wished that you could fly, you may be really talking about a feeling of freedom and unrestraint, or a wish to be lighter than air.) What is it about you or your lifestyle that made you wish what you did? Is there any way that you can bring those qualities into your life in a realistic manner?

Now think about how it felt to actually do this exercise. Were you comfortable dreaming? Did you find it easy to complete the sentence, did you feel silly, or did your mind go blank? If it was easy for you, ask yourself if it is also easy for you to dream in real life. Are you an idealist? Do you ever follow those dreams? Do you not only follow them, but also follow through with an effort to attain them?

If it was difficult for you to fantasize a response to this exercise, ask yourself why? Do you have a hard time casting off restrictions in other areas of your life? Do you ever take time to dream or play? Why or why not? Think about what these answers tell you about yourself.

EXERCISE 12: "I'm Afraid To..."

Think about the fear which you discussed in this exercise, and then think about any other fears that you might have. Are there any similarities between these fears? How are they connected to each other, if at all? Do you think that if you could conquer one of these fears, it would be easier to conquer the others?

Now think about the roots of your fears. What is the first time you remember feeling afraid of this thing? How do you think this fear came about? For example, if you are afraid of dogs, is it because you were once bitten by a dog? Or, have you heard a lot of stories about dogs hurting people? Or, do you just feel scared when you're near dogs, but don't really know why?

If the last example is your case, think about what else could be connected to this fear. Do big black dogs remind you of bears, which are a more powerful and frightening animal? Do you feel more afraid near very active dogs because they seem to be out of control? Are you afraid of being attacked or overpowered? Ask yourself questions such as these to try and determine the root of your fears.

INTERPRETATIONS: PHASE II (Chapter 11)

EXERCISE 1:   Things That Haunt Me

Look back over your list and see if you can find any connection between the things that haunt you. Are they alike in any way? Can you find any patterns in your list? What qualities do they have in common?

Think about the things on your list in more detail. If you wrote, "my childhood", as something that haunts you, try to be more specific. If you wrote, "my first love", ask yourself what exactly is it about your first love that haunts you.

Look for patterns again in these details. Then take some time to write about what these patterns mean to you. If everything on your list had something to do with the theme of loss, explore your feelings about that in more depth. If everything on the list was somehow connected to your friendships, then write about that.

Examine and think about how you deal with the things that haunt you. Do you ignore them? Confront them? Give them away?

EXERCISE 2:   Dreams

The more regularly you write about your dreams, the better you will be able to explore their possible meaning to you. Along with recording the content of your dreams, make it a point to jot down some facts about the events and feelings that you experienced during the day or week prior to your dream.

Use your daytime information in combination with your nighttime information to look for connections and patterns. Do the feelings in your dream mirror the feelings in your waking life? (If you are anxious about something during the day, are your dreams filled with anxious moments also?) Are there any patterns to your dreams in connection to your waking life? Do you always dream about your grandfather after a visit to your home town? Do you always dream about chaotic situations when you are tackling a new project at work?

One way to think about your dreams is to focus on the feelings behind them. What are you feeling towards the other characters in your dreams? What are you feeling in general? Do you feel in control or helpless when tackling a crisis situation? Do you feel embarrassed or confident when suddenly appearing in public without your clothes? (This is a common dream.) Do you feel warmth or animosity toward your family members or friends? Think about the relation of your dream feelings to your waking feelings. Your dreams may help you become aware of feelings that you hide from yourself during the day.

Finally, write about your own speculations as to the meaning of the dream. What do you think it was all about? What do you think it meant? Why do you think you dreamt this now?

(Please note: This exercise is not meant to be a lesson in dream interpretation, but only a stepping off point for you to begin thinking about your inner self.)

EXERCISE 3: Good-byes

You can learn something about yourself and your needs by examining your behavior patterns and feelings with regard to separation and loss. Look back at what you have written for this exercise. What are the patterns that you see? What is your usual reaction to a loss or separation? How do you take care of yourself at these times? Are you able to provide nurturing for yourself, or do you turn toward other people? Do you address the loss directly, or do you avoid or ignore it?

Try to find the specific ways that you deal well with loss or separation, and list them. Then look for the parts of a leave-taking that are the most difficult for you. Make a list of them, also. Review your two lists of strengths and weaknesses. Do these seem familiar to you? Do they parallel your behavior in other areas of your life?

Are there any parts of your life right now where a "good-bye" would be healthy, but you haven't yet said it? Think about what is holding you back. What are you afraid of? Write about your expectations.

EXERCISE 4: What Do I Look Like?

Read back over your response to this exercise as if you were an outside observer. What kind of an impression do you get from what you read? What kind of a person do you picture from the items that you have described? What do your physical surroundings tell you about yourself?

Is this the same impression that you have of yourself? Are you happy with this description? What things do you like, and what do you wish were different? Do you feel that the items you have used to describe yourself are really representative of who you are? If not, why not?

EXERCISE 5: Highs And Lows—A Graph Of Yourself

What is your first reaction when you look at your completed graph? Are there any surprises? Can you see any patterns in your highs and lows?

Look more carefully at your picture. What do the items placed above your neutral line have in common? What do the items placed below your neutral line have in common? Which side of the line has the most items?

Take some time to think about where your pleasures and irritations come from. Is the source of your highs or lows generally within you, or outside of you? What does this tell you about yourself?

EXERCISE 6: Take A Letter

If you have written a letter to another person, read back over it and underline the passages that you would not have said directly to this person. Then label the feelings that are connected to each passage. Think about why it is difficult for you to express these particular feelings to this particular person. Would it be just as difficult with someone else? Why or why not?

Think about how this information relates to the rest of your life. Why do you think it is difficult for you to express these feelings? When did you learn to be apprehensive about this? What would be at risk if these feelings were expressed directly?

If you have written a letter to yourself, read back over it. What have you revealed about yourself that you were not before aware of?

EXERCISE 7:   The Child Within

How easy was it to find the child within you?   Did you feel any resistance to leaving your adult self, or did you give it up without a struggle?   How far down did you have to dig to find the feelings and reactions of your little child?   Thinking about the answers to these questions will make you aware of how in touch you are with that inner part of yourself, and to what extent you have been trained to hide it.

Read over what your child expressed.   Label and list the feelings that you find.   Are you comfortable with these feelings? Do you ever express them in your daily life?   What do you do with them if you don't allow them expression?   Where did you learn to deal with your child in this way?

EXERCISE 8:   A Feeling Log

How many different feelings did you record as you completed this exercise?   Were you surprised that there were so many, or so few?   Which feelings did you experience most often?   Do you have a broad range of feelings, or is the scope limited?   Has it always been this way for you?

Look at the connections between your feelings and their precipitating events.   Do they make sense?   Are they logically combined?

Do your feelings tend to be extreme and deep, or less intense? Can you find any other patterns in your experience of feeling?   Are these patterns similar to those of either of your parents?   Did this exercise reveal anything about yourself that you were not previously aware of?   How had you hidden the information and why do you think you did?

EXERCISE 9: "If I Won The Lottery..."

Take a look at the different ways that you decided to spend your money. What do these choices tell you about your priorities? What do they tell you about your values? What do they tell you about your comfort level with taking risks?

Think about the way that you answered the questions in this exercise. Was it easy for you to decide how to spend this much money? What kinds of feelings did you have as you worked on this problem? What factors affected your final decisions? How much did you let other people influence your choices?

Are you working toward taking these financial steps (purchases, investments, trips, etc.) in your life even if you don't win the lottery? Why or why not?

EXERCISE 10: Some Things Never Change

Look back over your time chart and list of personal characteristics. Which traits have never changed and which have fluctuated? Why? Make another list categorizing the traits as "changeable" or "constant." Which list is longer? Think about why.

Ask yourself the reasons behind the changes in your personality. Then think about the motivations for the constant factors remaining the same. Have your reasons been mainly conscious or unconscious?

Look over your long-term chart. What patterns, if any, can you find? What was going on in your life when you did the most changing? At what times did you change the least?

EXERCISE 11: Family Tree

Begin examining your family tree by looking for patterns and repeated words. Did you use the same descriptive word for more than one person in your family?   Make a list of all the "descriptors" that you wrote on your mother's side of the tree, and another list of the words about your father's side. Compare the two. How are they alike and how are they different?

Now look at the words that you used to describe yourself. Do they fit more with your mother's side or your father's? (Or neither?) Do you share any common "descriptors" with anyone else in your family?

Put circles around the names of the people that you feel the closest to in your family. Compare their characteristics to each other, and then compare them to yours. How are they alike or different? What patterns do you see in your family characteristics or values? What can you learn about yourself by looking at those who came before you?

INTERPRETATIONS: PHASE III (Chapter 12)

EXERCISE 1: In the Beginning

Look at the earliest memories that you have written about. Do
they have anything in common? What kinds of feelings are
attached to them? Are they all significant events, or daily events?
Do they all carry the same feelings, or do they represent a variety
of emotional states? What kinds of patterns do you see in the
memories of your early childhood? Think not only about events,
but also feelings and relationships.

Next, think about how easy or difficult it was for you to
complete this exercise. Did your memories come back easily? Or
was it hard to remember? Are there long blocks of time for which
you have no memory at all? Think about why that might be. If
possible, talk with friends or relatives who could fill in the missing
spaces.

The events, people, and experiences in a person's early
childhood will affect the type of person that they become. Your
first relationships teach you to either trust or mistrust the world; to
feel control over meeting your needs, or to feel helpless; and to
establish a sense of self and individuality. How did your earliest
experiences affect who you are today?

EXERCISE 2: A Present To Yourself

How did you feel inside as you worked on this exercise? Was
it a pleasant experience, or uncomfortable? Did you feel
deserving, or guilty? How do your answers to these questions

coincide with the way you experience the rest of your life?

Do you regularly practice nurturing yourself by using positive feedback in this way? If not, how do you nurture yourself? What do you use to give yourself pats on the back?

Was it easy or difficult for you to think of yourself as your own best friend? If it was difficult, think about why. How do you feel about the thought of being a friend to yourself? How would you treat yourself if you were your own best friend?

EXERCISE 3: Point of View

The great value in broadening your perspective and being able to see things from another point of view is that you will increase your ability to foster and sustain healthy relationships, both in the workplace and in your personal life. The ability for healthy conflict resolution is increased as your ability to see things from the other person's point of view is increased. Hopefully, also, the better you can see things from another's point of view, the better you will be able to see yourself.

What happened as you tried to describe yourself from another person's point of view? Was it difficult at first? Were you able to better understand that other person's actions toward you when you were seeing yourself through their eyes? Were you better able to understand their feelings toward you when you put yourself in their position?

Look at what you have written. Which places did you have the easiest time seeing through the other person's eyes? In which places did you have the hardest time? Why do you think that is? What does this tell you about your vulnerabilities and your defenses?

EXERCISE 4: Dialogue

This exercise allows you to learn something about yourself and your situation by listening to yourself and others speak. Observing the words that you have put into the characters' mouths will teach you about your own point of view on both the speakers and the situation. When you dialogue with yourself the benefits double.

Look first at your choice of characters. Why did you choose these particular ones? Was there something that you needed to work out between them? Or, were they neutral beings, providing a "safe" conversation with which to start?

Did you choose yourself as one of the speakers? Why or why not? Was it easier to write from yourself than from the other character, or vice versa? Did you reveal anything in your dialogue that you weren't planning to say? Or did you reveal anything that you hadn't known about your characters before?

What feelings were expressed in your dialogue? What feelings were not expressed? Why did you leave those out? What can you tell about your feelings for your characters by the words you have put into their mouths? Do you think this conversation could ever really take place? What wishes did you fulfill by creating this conversation?

EXERCISE 5: This Is How I Look Today

How did it feel to focus on your "inner picture" instead of your other presentation? Did it seem odd or normal to picture yourself through your feelings rather than your looks? What does your answer tell you about your priorities and the roots of your self-image?

Look back at the items that you chose to include in your drawing. You chose these particular parts to depict and not others. Why are they the most important to you right now? What significance do these parts have to you? What about the parts that you left out?

Look at the size of your drawing. How big are you in relation to the paper? Where did you place yourself on the page? Think about these choices in relation to your self-image. Is your drawing in proportion? Or are some parts bigger than others? Ask yourself why. Are there certain parts that are colored in? Parts drawn more darkly? Parts with more or less detail? Think about the reasons behind this.

EXERCISE 6: Family Portrait

The first thing to look for in your family portrait is yourself. Did you include yourself? If not, think about why. Next, look at the positioning of your family members. Who did you draw next to whom? Who did you place the closest to you? Who did you place the furthest from you? Are there any family members that you left out? What are your feelings for them?

Look at the size of the figures in your picture. Are they all about the same size? Or are some bigger or smaller than the others? Why? What size are you compared to the rest of your family?

If you drew a picture with friends, ask yourself the same

questions. Also, which friends did you choose and which did you exclude? Where did you place yourself in the picture with your friends? How well does your picture represent reality?

Think of your drawing as a physical representation of your feelings about these people in your life. What does the picture tell you? Is it accurate? If not, why not? What does your picture tell you about your relationship with these other people?

EXERCISE 7: The Editor

Think about the feeling of control you had when doing this exercise. You had the power to change your life circumstances, to overpower the things that you were afraid of. How did that feel to you?

Think about what is keeping you from having that same control in your real life. What are the obstacles to overcoming your fears? What keeps you from making the changes that you desire? Who or what is in control of your outcomes, if not yourself? Are the answers to these questions surprises, or are they part of a repeating pattern in your life? When did the pattern start? What is preventing it from changing?

Think about what would happen if you had the same control over your real life as you were given in this exercise. Realistically, what would you edit in the story of your life as it is taking place in the present? Without being given a "magic" power, what steps would you have to take to make those changes?

EXERCISE 8: On Your Own

How much would your life change if your parents moved to Mars? Read back over your response to this exercise, and look at the kinds of changes that would take place in your life. What are they related to? Are they major or minor changes? Do they concern your job, looks, hobbies, family, friendships, living situation, the way you spend your time, or the way you spend your money?

Look at the degree to which your life would change. What does this tell you about the way you are living your life now?

Read back over the feelings you expressed in reaction to this announcement. Were they singular or mixed? Were they strong or ambivalent? Did they surprise you at all? What does your reaction tell you about the way you are connected to your parents today?

EXERCISE 9: "If I Were..."

Look back over your exercise. Is there a difference between the animal or food that your personality would make you and the animal or food that you wished to be? Why does that discrepancy exist? How do you feel about it?

Compare your chosen animals to your foods. Do they seem to fit together. (For example, if you thought you would become a panther and a corn flake, do these things seem to have the same or different qualities to you?) If they are not similar, try to figure out why.

Make a list of the characteristics that you would assign to each of your animal and food choices. What do these traits tell you about how you view your personality?

EXERCISE 10: Role Models

If you have siblings, it is likely that you had the same parents, grandparents, maybe teachers, and thus, at least one or two of the same role models. Compare your life and your personality to your sister's or brother's. How did you react differently or similarly to the same role models? What is it in your personality that caused you to imitate or reject certain traits of your role models, and your siblings to imitate or reject others?

What traits did you find similar or different in your role models compared to your heroes? What feelings do you have for your role models? What feelings do you have for your heroes? If your heroes are different from your role models, how do these changes reflect your own personal growth?

What values do your role models hold? What values do your heroes hold? How do each of these compare to your values as an adult?

EXERCISE 11: Never Say Never

Look back over the characteristics of this scenario that would never happen. What does your rejection of these things tell you about yourself and the way that you have chosen to live? What kind of a person are you? What do you value? What are your priorities?

What else does this thing that would never happen tell you

about yourself? What are your fears? What do you avoid in life? Think why. How did you come to be this way?

What did you discover about yourself in the second part of the exercise? How did you handle this unusual situation? Were you able to stretch yourself further than you had thought you would be able? Or did you become immobilized? Did you try to deal with the situation yourself, or did you turn to others for help? Was this reaction typical of the way you handle things in your normal daily life? What does this tell you about your dependence or your connectedness to others? What does it tell you about what you believe about the world?

EXERCISE 12: Looking Ahead

How easy was it for you to begin this exercise? Did you have trouble allowing yourself to imagine such a thing? Or did the fantasy come easily to you? Is this reaction typical of your personality?

As you read over your ideal day fantasy, make a list of the characteristics of a person in this situation. What are their values? Their priorities? Does this sound like you? Or does it sound like someone else—if so, who?

How does your ideal day compare to a day in your life right now? Make a list of the differences, and the similarities. Which list is longer? Why? Do you think your ideal day could actually be achieved? Why or why not? How do you feel about that? What other feelings do you have when you look into the future like this?

EXERCISE 13: Decisions, Decisions

Look over the list of reasons behind your major life decisions. Are all of your motivations the same? Or are they different? For example, did you make every decision based on your commitment to your family, or your desire to make money, or your need for variety and change, or your need for stability? Or, did you make different decisions for different reasons? What patterns do you see in your reasons for the decisions that you made? What do these patterns tell you about yourself?

Did your motivations for doing things change or remain the same over your life span? Do you make choices today the same way that you did five or ten years ago?

How many of your decisions are head-oriented, and how many are heart-oriented? (Which did you make because it was "wise", and which did you make because if "felt right"? Are they all one way or another? Or does it depend on the situation? Is this the way you typically think of yourself? How well has this decision-making process served you throughout your life?

15 NEVER-ENDINGS— SOME PARTING WORDS

Just as with every other facet of journal-writing, the amount of time in your life that you choose to keep a journal is also flexible, and solely up to you. You may choose to journal for a few days, a few weeks, several months, or several years. You may decide that you want to keep up your personal writing for the rest of your life, or you may wish to bring out your journal only at problem-solving times.

I recently pulled my junior high and high school diaries out of the attic and read them over from cover to cover. What an incredible experience—to be able to relive a portion of my life, day by day, through my own words. Reading those diaries brought back memories, brought perspective, and allowed me to experience a greater understanding of the girl that I had been, which I was never able to see at the time I was living those diary pages.

After reading my diaries, and realizing what a wealth of self-knowledge they held within their covers, I wished that I had continued them longer. I would have liked the opportunity to go back to any day of any year in my life and see what was happening then, to remember what I was feeling, and to recall what the world looked like to me back at that time.

But I didn't continue my daily diaries, because as I grew and changed they were no longer needed. Their purpose had been filled. Today I keep a journal, writing sporadically, as the need arises. I won't try to go back to daily diary-writing, because that's not what I need today. My journal, however, will be with me for as long as I live. Whenever the need does arise, I know that I can pick it up and keep going right where I left off—keep observing, assessing, working through, and pushing ahead. It is a tool to help me to keep growing, to be with me on my journey.

You may want to keep your journal until you complete the exercises in this book. You may want to keep it until you do each of them twice. You may want to get to a point where your struggles are lighter, or where you behavior has changed, or where your awareness has been fine-tuned. The distance you decide to take your journal-writing is up to you.

Whether or not you choose to continue journaling, I hope that you always continue your journey. For as long as you continue to search and question and take just one more step, you will continue to grow, and to become more and more of who you were created to become. The opportunity for growth is always present, you need only to be open to it. My eighth grade math teacher wrote something in my autograph book that, as a thirteen year-old, I didn't yet understand. He wrote, "Lisa, Dare to be..."

> *"Reading back over my journal, I saw so much—so much depth...pain, happiness, uncertainty, and on and on. It was so full. A full emotional life. I want that. I don't want to walk away from anything because it's hard."*
> *-Claire*

> *"After traveling for three days, I've been able to do some thinking about the year. I started out so low, so down, terrified of new situations, of being alone, of new people, of having no close friends. And here it is a year later and*

nothing was so bad as I expected. After starting out so intolerant I think I have learned tolerance. I believe I've become more open-minded. I have lost my pure liberal attitude, although I'm not sure it was all mine, or ever mine, or just a part of who I was with. I realize I have come full circle. I have found the middle ground I was searching for. I think, in fact, I am living in reality."
-Abby

"I feel good! What does it feel like to feel good? It's a free feeling—like I'm lighter; I can fly high because there is less weighing me down. It's a singing of the soul—a joy and enjoyment of who I am and what is around me."
-Jenny

"Today I wanted to climb up to the top of the hill and just sit and meditate, and I started to walk up the hill away from town. I looked around and realized that even when I got to the top of this hill, there were other hills that were higher, and mountains that were higher still. It wasn't like these were far away either. All I had to do to see them was to turn around. And I realized then that life is going to be like that—no matter how good I get at something, there's always a higher mountain." -Erin